LATEX, concisely

ELLIS HORWOOD SERIES IN COMPUTERS AND THEIR APPLICATIONS
Series Editor: IAN CHIVERS, Senior Analyst, The Computer Centre, King's College, London, and formerly Senior Programmer and Analyst, Imperial College of Science and Technology, University of London

Abramsky, S. & Hankin, C.J.	ABSTRACT INTERPRETATION OF DECLARATIVE LANGUAGES
Alexander, H.	FORMALLY-BASED TOOLS AND TECHNIQUES FOR HUMAN–COMPUTER DIALOGUES
Anderson, J.	MODEL-BASED COMPUTER VISION: A Synthesised Approach
Atherton, R.	STRUCTURED PROGRAMMING WITH COMAL
Baeza-Yates, R.A.	TEXT SEARCHING ALGORITHMS
Bailey, R.	FUNCTIONAL PROGRAMMING WITH HOPE
Barrett, R., Ramsay, A. & Sloman, A.	POP-11
Beardon, C., Lumsden, D. & Holmes, G.	NATURAL LANGUAGE AND COMPUTATIONAL LINGUISTICS: An Introduction
Berztiss, A.	PROGRAMMING WITH GENERATORS
Bharath, R.	COMPUTERS AND GRAPH THEORY: Representing Knowledge for Processing by Computers
Bishop, P.	FIFTH GENERATION COMPUTERS
Brierley, B. & Kemble, I.	COMPUTERS AS A TOOL IN LANGUAGE TEACHING
Britton, C.	THE DATABASE PROBLEM: A Practitioner's Guide
Bullinger, H.-J. & Gunzenhauser, H.	SOFTWARE ERGONOMICS
Burns, A.	NEW INFORMATION TECHNOLOGY
Carberry, J.C.	COBOL
de Carlini, U. & Villano, U.	TRANSPUTERS AND PARALLEL ARCHITECTURES
Chivers, I.D. & Sleighthome, J.	INTERACTIVE FORTRAN 77: A Hands on Approach 2nd Edition
Clark, M.W.	PC-PORTABLE FORTRAN
Clark, M.W.	TEX
Cockshott, W.P.	A COMPILER WRITER'S TOOLBOX: How to Implement Interactive Compilers for PCs with Turbo Pascal
Cockshott, W.P.	PS-ALGOL IMPLEMENTATIONS: Applications in Persistent Object-Oriented Programming
Colomb, R.M.	IMPLEMENTING PERSISTENT PROLOG: Large, Dynamic, Shared Procedures in Prolog
Cooper, M.	VISUAL OCCLUSION AND THE INTERPRETATION OF AMBIGUOUS PICTURES
Cope, T	COMPUTING USING BASIC
Curth, M.A. & Edelmann, H.	APL
Dahlstrand, I.	SOFTWARE PORTABILITY AND STANDARDS
Dah Ming Chiu, & Sudama, R.	NETWORK MONITORING EXPLAINED: Design and Application
Dandamudi, S.P.	HIERARCHICAL HYPERCUBE MULTICOMPUTER INTERCONNECTION NETWORKS
Dongarra, J., Duff, I., Gaffney, P., & McKee, S.	VECTOR AND PARALLEL COMPUTING
Drop, R.	WORKING WITH dBASE LANGUAGES
Dunne, P.E.	COMPUTABILITY THEORY: Concepts and Applications
Eastlake, J.J.	A STRUCTURED APPROACH TO COMPUTER STRATEGY
Eisenbach, S.	FUNCTIONAL PROGRAMMING
Ellis, D.	MEDICAL COMPUTING AND APPLICATIONS
Ennals, J.R.	ARTIFICIAL INTELLIGENCE
Ennals, J.R., *et al.*	INFORMATION TECHNOLOGY AND EDUCATION
Fillipic, B.	PROLOG USER'S HANDBOOK
Ford, N.	COMPUTER PROGRAMMING LANGUAGES
Ford, N.J., Ford, J.M., Holman, D.F. & Woodroffe, M.R.	COMPUTERS AND COMPUTER APPLICATIONS: An Introduction for the 1990s
Ford, N. & Ford, J.	INTRODUCING FORMAL METHODS: A Less Mathematical Approach
Gray, P.M.D.	LOGIC, ALGEBRA AND DATABASES
Grill, E.	RELATIONAL DATABASES
Grune, D. & Jacobs, C.J.H.	PARSING TECHNIQUES: A Practical Guide
Guariso, G. & Werthner, H.	ENVIRONMENTAL DECISION SUPPORT SYSTEMS
Harland, D.M.	CONCURRENCY AND PROGRAMMING LANGUAGES
Harland, D.M.	POLYMORPHIC PROGRAMMING LANGUAGES
Harland, D.M.	REKURSIV
Henshall, J. & Shaw, S.	OSI EXPLAINED, 2nd Edition
Hepburn, P.H.	FURTHER PROGRAMMING IN PROLOG
Hepburn, P.H.	PROGRAMMING IN MICRO-PROLOG MADE SIMPLE
Hill, I.D. & Meek, B.L.	PROGRAMMING LANGUAGE STANDARDISATION
Hirschheim, R., Smithson, S. & Whitehouse, D.	MICROCOMPUTERS AND THE HUMANITIES: Survey and Recommendations
Hutchins, W.J.	MACHINE TRANSLATION
Hutchison, D.	FUNDAMENTALS OF COMPUTER LOGIC
Hutchison, D. & Silvester, P.	COMPUTER LOGIC
Johnstone, A.	LATEX CONCISELY
Kirkwood, J.	HIGH PERFORMANCE RELATIONAL DATABASE DESIGN

Series continued at back of book

LATEX, concisely

ADRIAN JOHNSTONE
Department of Computer Science, Royal Holloway and
Bedford New College, University of London

ELLIS HORWOOD
NEW YORK   LONDON   TORONTO   SYDNEY   TOKYO   SINGAPORE

First published in 1992 by
ELLIS HORWOOD LIMITED
Market Cross House, Cooper Street,
Chichester, West Sussex, PO19 1EB, England

A division of
Simon & Schuster International Group
A Paramount Communications Company

Printed and bound in Great Britain
by Redwood, Melksham

British Library Cataloguing in Publication Data

A catalogue record for this book is available from the British Library

ISBN 0–13–524539–7 Pbk

Library of Congress Cataloging-in-Publication Data

Available from the publisher

This book was typeset using LaTeX and the Computer Modern fonts. Camera-ready copy
was prepared using the University of London Computer Centre typesetter service.

Amiga is a trademark of Commodore Business Machines,
IBM is a tademark of International Business Machines,
Macintosh is a trademark of Apple Computers,
MS-DOS is a trademark of Microsoft,
Postscript is a trademark of Adobe Systems,
TeX is a trademark of the American Mathematical Society,
Unix is a trademark of AT&T,
VMS is a trademark of Digital Equipment Corporation.

Contents

List of Figures

List of Tables

Preface

The book is written for people who already have some familiarity with computers and want a short overview of LaTeX. To that end, I have attempted to introduce features in the order in which they might be required by someone learning the system, and give a complete treatment of their capabilities in a single pass. The main aim is to cover all of LaTeX's features in as concise a fashion as possible, presenting concentrated information in a small book affordable by students.

A secondary aim is to give an understanding of the processes underlying LaTeX's operation as a guide to the writer of style files. Many people find that LaTeX is easy to use for straightforward tasks, but can be obstructive if one wants to change the details of page layout. This has given LaTeX the quite undeserved reputation of being a tool for neophytes only. In particular, many `plain` TeX users refuse to have anything to do with it because they claim that they simply *can't* do some things. This is a shame, because some of LaTeX's basic facilities (such as cross referencing and automatic table of contents generation) are so useful that `plain` TeX users are almost bound to end up implementing them themselves or doing the job by hand.

It turns out that LaTeX is malleable, but TeX code is often very difficult to read, and the LaTeX source code runs to hundreds of pages, so most users admit defeat and put up with the standard styles. As a result, many LaTeX documents look similar which is a waste of a fine typesetting system. However, if you persevere, you will find that modifying an existing style file is quite straightforward.

A word of warning is in order here. The title of this book is 'LaTeX, *concisely*' and *concise* is not a synonym for *precise*. It is inevitable that much detail, especially concerning internals, is missing. However, my own experience of teaching LaTeX users is that given enough help to overcome the initial opaqueness of style file source code they can progress to make changes as they need them. I have concentrated on making common adjustments to existing styles rather than attempting a grand overview of how to program TeX and LaTeX. A comprehensive explanation would surely run to several volumes, and other authors are far more qualified than I for such a task.

Prefaces usually finish with some acknowledgements, but I would like to make some apologies as well. Most of all I would like to apologise to Phil Taylor, our local TeX guru, who firmly believes that all TeX users should stick to `plain` TeX. He will almost certainly be appalled to learn that this book could not have been written without his help. I should also apologise to my students, who have been waiting for this expanded edition for two years. I am indebted to many people for the help they have given me either directly, or indirectly by the provision of excellent software tools. In particular, I would like to thank Peter Hoare and Dave Whiteland (who drew some of the figures for me), and the support staff and my academic colleagues at Royal Holloway, University of London, King's College London and Curtin University of Technology, Western Australia.

In the process of writing this book I have used six different TeX implementations running on three different operating systems, and on a variety of machines ranging in size from a room down to a book. The dedication of the small army of TeX implementers and maintainers in providing public domain software of such an astoundingly high standard is truly remarkable. Knuth and Lamport's altruism in placing their original work in the public domain would probably seem incomprehensible to anyone outside of the computing profession. Let us hope that this tradition of sharing long continues.

In real life I design computer hardware and integrated circuits so perhaps I should be blasé, but the rate of technological progress never ceases to amaze me. The final copy of this book was typeset on a notebook computer little larger than the printed text and it ran about fifteen times faster than my first TeX system. Apart from the extraordinary increase in speed, my notebook computer allowed me to typeset in the garden, and so my final acknowledgement is to Jennifer, who provided the garden.

June 1992

1

First examples

TeX is a computer typesetting system written by Professor Donald Knuth of Stanford University. It can produce books, letters and articles typeset to the highest standards. TeX is not a 'word processor' — you prepare TeX input files using a separate text editor. The input file consists of the text you want to appear on the printed page interspersed with formatting commands which specify how the text is to be typeset. The actual spacing and layout of the source file does not necessarily reflect the spacing of the printed page. This is in contrast to word processors which often try to give a visual indication of the printed output whilst you are typing.

The TeX program itself provides about 300 'primitive commands', which as their name suggests are rather low level. Describing a document using these primitives would be time consuming and error prone. TeX therefore offers a way of creating new commands of arbitrary complexity by defining *macros*.

A macro is a single command that is shorthand for a sequence of other commands. When TeX encounters a macro it simply replaces it with the underlying sequence of commands — an operation referred to as *macro expansion*. Some of these commands might be macros too, so the process continues until all the macros have been expanded to a list of primitives.

1.1 TeX and LaTeX

In the TeXbook [Knu86a] Knuth describes a set of macros that equip TeX with a more high level set of commands. This package is called `plain` TeX. Although it is much easier to use than primitive TeX it still leaves many design decisions to the user and as a result most people build up their own sets of macros to enhance `plain` to their own personal requirements. This is a blessing and a curse — on the one hand you get exactly the visual effects you want, but on the other you have to learn rather a lot about TeX's internals to write a good set of macros. It turns out that macro expansion languages exhibit rather subtle (i.e. confusing) behaviour, and writing powerful and general macros can be very time consuming.

LaTeX is an alternative (and much larger) set of macros for TeX that has capabilities similar to the Unix `troff` system and the VMS Runoff program. It will automatically build a table of contents, list of figures and an index. It has a rather powerful mechanism for describing tables, and it can even draw simple pictures. The system was originally described in the LaTeX book [Lam86] written by Leslie Lamport, the author of LaTeX.

Presently the world of TeX users divides into roughly two camps — those who use `plain` and 'roll their own' high level macros, and those who use LaTeX. (In fact this is an insulting over-simplification: there are a number of other alternative macro packages, especially $\mathcal{AMS}$-TeX which is popular with mathematicians. However, LaTeX and `plain` are distributed with nearly all TeX systems, whereas these other packages have to be acquired separately, limiting their use to those who actively seek them out. You will find more information on other macro packages in Chapter 13.)

As a matter of fact LaTeX is built on top of a slightly modified version of `plain` so you might think that the two packages would be compatible with each other. Sadly this is not so. Most of `plain` will work within LaTeX but important parts do not. In addition, it is easy to upset LaTeX's internal definitions by careless use of `plain` commands.

In retrospect, it seems unfortunate that the full `plain` command set was not left embedded within LaTeX. Many `plain` TeX users refuse to have anything to do with LaTeX because they claim that their own macros will not work, and also that LaTeX forces their documents into a certain style. The former is probably true (although conversion of many macros is trivial), the latter is not. LaTeX is easy to customise, but unfortunately the LaTeX book provides little advice on how to go about it.

1.2   Customising LaTeX

The central idea in LaTeX is to use a single set of commands to define the logical flow of the document (in terms of chapter headings, definition of tables and so on) and then have a separate set of definitions called a *style* that specifies how the logical units should actually appear on the page. That way the process of producing logically structured text is separated from the visual design of the finished document.

The macro definitions making up the document style are usually kept in a separate file called a *style file*. Four standard styles are distributed with LaTeX — `book`, `report`, `article` and `letter`. This book has been formatted using a modified version of `book` which produces documents to the Ellis Horwood house style.

Since all of the visual formatting information is kept is a separate file named at the beginning of the document file, wholesale changes can be made to the look of the printed document file (including changing the size of the type and the size of the printed page) with a single change to the source file.

It is important to resist the temptation to put specific visual formatting commands into your document. Sometimes it is necessary — some of the tables in this book have been specially balanced for the Ellis Horwood size pages and would need adjusting for a smaller or larger page for instance, but by and large you should never specify where exactly on a page an item is to go. If you want to change the look of your document you should write a new style file which in most cases need be only a slightly modified version of one of the standard styles. Chapter 11 describes LaTeX's visual formatting parameters, and Chapter 12 describes how to obtain commonly requested effects by modifying the standard styles.

It is quite likely that at some stage you will run up against a die-hard `plain` TeX user who will sneer at you for using LaTeX and tell you that he can, for instance, put equation numbers just where he wants them. Well so can you, but he may not believe it. If you run up against such a zealot then treat them with courtesy, perhaps even sympathy, but do not allow them to distract you from getting your job done.

1.3   A note on pronunciation

Having dispensed with the politics, the next pressing question is how to pronounce 'LaTeX'. Knuth is quite clear in the TeXbook that TeX is an uppercase form of the Greek $\tau\epsilon\chi$, meaning art as well as technology. Hence it should be pronounced *teck*, where the *-ck* should be like the final 'ch' in the Scottish loch. It is a sound that does not really occur in English, and so many people approximate it to *-k*, giving *tek*. Whatever you do, don't pronounce χ as an X (*teks*) or you will receive pitying smiles from those in the know.

Deciding on the pronunciation of 'LaTeX' is a little more difficult because Lamport declined to specify it on the basis that '...pronunciation is best determined by usage, not fiat'. Round here people say *lay*-teck although I know one person who says *lah*-teck.

1.4   A first example

When you meet a new computer language (and TeX is a language, although not a very general purpose one) the first thing to do is to write a program that outputs `Hello world!` and get it to run. To make LaTeX typeset and print out a message you should perform the following four steps.

(The commands required for steps 2–4 vary from computer to computer. If you are working on a large computer installation then you should ask another user or the system manager what to do. If you are running on a personal computer then look in the manuals for your TeX system or ask the person who installed TeX. Appendix A gives hints for using several TeX systems running on Unix, MS-DOS and VMS.)

1. Use a text editor to create a file called `world.tex` containing these lines:

   ```
   \documentstyle{article}
   \begin{document}
   Hello world!
   \end{document}
   ```

2. Run LaTeX on `world.tex`

   When you run LaTeX on `world.tex` you should see messages similar to these appearing on your screen

   ```
   This is TeX, Version 3.0
   (WORLD.TEX
   LaTeX Version 2.09 <18 March 1992>
   ```

```
(ARTICLE.STY
Standard Document Style 'article'. <14 Jan 92>
(ART10.STY))
No file WORLD.aux.
[1] (WORLD.AUX)
Output written on WORLD.DVI (1 page, 232 bytes).
Transcript written on WORLD.LOG.
```

The messages you see are likely to differ in detail from these. The dates in angle brackets give the release dates of this version of LaTeX. (If the dates you see are earlier than mid-1991, you should consider updating your system.) The filenames may appear differently depending on the computer you are using. Don't worry about these minor differences, but if you see messages like

```
! Undefined control sequence.
l.1 \documntstyle
                 {article}
?
```

or

```
LaTeX error.  See LaTeX manual for explanation.
              Type  H <return>  for immediate help.
! Missing \begin{document}.
?
```

then you have an error. After printing the question mark, TeX will stop and wait for instructions. You will find advice on how to interpret TeX's error messages in Appendix B, but for now just type X in response to the question mark. This causes TeX to eXit so that you can re-edit the file `world.tex` and fix your spelling error.

At the end of the run you will find two new files `world.dvi` and `world.log`[1]. The `log` file contains a copy of all the messages that appear on your screen during the run, sometimes with extra information. The `dvi` file is a *device-independent* description of your document that makes no assumptions about the kind of printer you will be using.

3. Run a *DVI driver*

A DVI driver is a program that takes the `.dvi` file and translates it into a printable file for a specific printer. TeX uses the graphics capability of the printer to draw the characters rather than simply using the manufacturer supplied characters. There are many different ways of describing graphics commands to printers, and therefore many different DVI drivers are required.

---

[1]On VMS and some other operating systems this file is called `world.lis` to avoid confusion with batch log files

Most DVI drivers have a multitude of options to select which pages are to be printed (useful if you want to check a single change in a large document) and in some cases to print two pages side by side at reduced magnification (and hence reduced quality) on a single sheet, which helps save paper if you just want a draft printout. It would be a good idea to obtain a copy of the manual for your DVI driver. Often it is available as a DVI file, so you can use the driver to print the documentation[2].

4. Send the output of the driver to the printer. Sometimes the operating system print command is used but usually some special command is required. On some systems, the DVI driver automatically sends its output to the printer, so this step may not be needed at all.

When you have successfully completed these stages you will get something that looks like the example shown on page 6. Just to prove to yourself that there is no relationship between the format of `world.tex` and the resulting output, try editing `world.tex` and putting all the commands on a single line thus:

```
\documentstyle{article}\begin{document}Hello world!\end{document}
```

Run the file through steps 1–4 again and verify that the typeset output is the same.

1.5   A large example

The rest of this chapter is a sort of overture to the main book. The idea is to familiarise you with LaTeX commands by showing you an example document that exercises many LaTeX features and show you the typeset output and the source file side-by-side. The actual text of the example is meant to be read too — it contains hints on how to avoid simple errors, and when to use some features.

All of the commands in the example are described in detail later in the book. A good way to get started in LaTeX is to use the structure of this example as a template for your own documents. If you do not understand how a particular effect was created, look at the corresponding part of the source file and then look up those commands in the index to this book.

1.5.1   Preliminaries

The paragraphs in a LaTeX file are separated by blank lines. Most LaTeX commands are introduced with a \ character. A few commands generate text directly, such as the command `\today` which will insert the date of the run into your typeset output.

Some commands are *declarations* and do not actually produce any output text, rather they redefine the way the text is to be produced. For instance, the declaration `\bf` causes the following text to be set in a **bold font**.

Curly braces { and } are used to create *groups*. Any declarations made inside a group will be forgotten at the end of the group, so the commands

---

[2]Of course there is a nasty chicken and egg problem here — how will you know how to print the manual without reading it first? Answer: ask someone else who uses your LaTeX system.

Hello world!

```
some {\bf bold} text
```
produces
some **bold** text

because the effect of the \bf declaration is reset at the end of the group.

Many commands take *parameters* which are placed in braces after the command name. For instance the command \underline{A} produces A. Some commands take more than one parameter. There are commands that take *optional parameters* which may be omitted, in which case LaTeX will take some default action. Optional parameters are marked with brackets [and] instead of braces.

This book uses a special font to typeset fragments of LaTeX code.

> Text like this represents LaTeX instructions that you can type in directly.

> *Text in italics* represents a LaTeX part-of-speech that you must replace with a specific name or piece of text.

For instance, elsewhere in this book you will be told that the command

```
\underline{text}
```

causes *text* to be typeset with underlining. You can type anything you like (including other LaTeX commands[3]) instead of *text*, but you must type the \underline and the braces as shown.

Commands of the form

```
\begin{environment name} ... \end{environment name}
```

define the start and end of *environments* and must be paired. Within an environment some special layout will be used to typeset your text. For instance, any text between a \begin{center} and an \end{center} is centred on the page. (Note the American spelling of center here.) Any declarations made within an environment will be forgotten after the corresponding \end command, just as they would be at the end of a group. Groups and environments may be nested.

All LaTeX document files must have the same basic form as the world.tex file. There must be exactly one \documentstyle{style}, one \begin{document} and one \end{document} command in that order. The part of the document file before the \begin{document} is called the *preamble*. No text is produced by the preamble, and blank lines are ignored. Text generating commands are in fact illegal in the preamble, which must include only declarations, such as the title of the document. Some declarations may *only* appear in the preamble. Many documents (such as world.tex) have empty preambles because the default formatting is acceptable.

Rather a lot of technical terms have been defined in this section. Chapter 2 discusses these in more detail. For now, if some of the terminology seems obscure then it is best to simply plough on, using the example file to guide you and looking up commands in the index as you meet them.

---

[3]Some commands may place restrictions on what other commands you may use inside their parameters.

A LaTeX document

Adrian Johnstone[*]

June 1992

Abstract

This document contains examples of many LaTeX features. It is taken from Chapter 1 of 'LaTeX, *concisely*'.

1   Introduction

TeX is a computer program for typesetting papers and books. LaTeX is a package of *macros* that add features such as cross referencing, table of contents generation and automatic compilation of bibliographies. It is designed to feel rather like systems such as the Unix[1] `troff` and VMS[2] Runoff packages.

Auxiliary programs help in making sorted bibliographies, indices and glossaries. You should also find out if a spelling checker is available on your computerr.

1.1   A subsection

LaTeX provides *sectioning* commands for parts, chapters, sections, subsections, subsubsections and others. It will automatically keep track of section numbers and generate a table of contents for you.

---

[*]Computer Science Department, Royal Holloway, University of London
[1]Unix is a trademark of AT&T
[2]VMS is a trademark of Digital Equipment Co.

1

```
\documentstyle{article}

%This is a comment.
%A comment is everything after a % sign up to the end of line.

\setlength{\textheight}{160mm}    %To fit Ellis Horwood
\setlength{\textwidth}{115mm}     %To fit Ellis Horwood

\title{A \LaTeX\ document} \author{Adrian Johnstone% ignore eol
\thanks{Computer Science Department, Royal Holloway, University
of London}} \date{June 1992}

% End of preamble

\begin{document} %Start of real document
\maketitle

\begin{abstract}This document contains examples of many \LaTeX\
features. It is taken from Chapter 1 of `\LaTeX, {\em
concisely}'.\end{abstract}

\section{Introduction}

\TeX\ is a computer program for typesetting papers and books.
\LaTeX\ is a package of {\em macros} that add features such as
cross referencing, table of contents generation and automatic
compilation of bibliographies. It is designed to feel rather like
systems such as the Unix\footnote{Unix is a trademark of AT\&T}
{\tt troff} and VMS\footnote{VMS is a trademark of Digital
Equipment Co.} Runoff packages.

Auxiliary programs help in making sorted bibliographies, indices
and glossaries. You should also find out if a spelling checker is
available on your computerr.

\subsection{A subsection} \LaTeX\ provides {\em sectioning}
commands for parts, chapters, sections, subsections,
subsubsections and others. It will automatically keep track of
section numbers and generate a table of contents for you.
```

An unnumbered subsection

If you follow the sectioning command with a * then the number is suppressed, and no table of contents entry is generated.

Many commands have *-forms that slightly modify their behaviour.

2   Things to watch when you are typing

Usually a LaTeX document will mostly be straight text with only occasional embedded formatting commands (this document has a very high proportion of formatting commands because it is designed to show off many features). However, even in straight text there are certain things you should watch for because typeset text is not the same as normal computer printout.

- words are separated by one or more spaces, but LaTeX makes its own decisions as to how to space the output. So it doesn't matter how many spaces you type.

- paragraphs are separated by one or more blank lines.

- don't use the keyboard double quote character ". Your keyboard has single left quote ' and single right quote ' keys. Reported speech is usually surrounded by double quote marks "thus". Reported speech within reported speech, and the first novel use of a technical term is usually surrounded by single quotes: "He said 'don't quote me on that'".

- TeX breaks lines by looking for interword spaces and sometimes by hyphenating. You can make an unbreakable interword space with a *tie* which is written ~ ensuring that the Mr in Mr Smith is never orphaned. You can disable line breaking altogether (including hyphenation) by putting text in a box which will simply hang out into the margin.

- You have already seen examples of *emphasized words* typeset in italic. *Emphasis* within *emphasis is shown in* Roman *type. But don't overdo it.*[1]

---

[1] This is a footnote to the emphasized text. Note the use of an italic correction to place the footnote mark correctly.

```
\subsection*{An unnumbered subsection} If you follow the
sectioning command with a {\tt *} then the number is suppressed,
and no table of contents entry is generated.

Many commands have {\tt *-}forms that slightly modify their
behaviour.

\section{Things to watch when you are typing} Usually a \LaTeX\
document will mostly be straight text with only occasional
embedded formatting commands (this document has a very high
proportion of formatting commands because it is designed to show
off many features). However, even in straight text there are
certain things you should watch for because typeset text is not
the same as normal computer printout.

\begin{itemize}

\item words are separated by one or more spaces, but \LaTeX\
makes its own decisions as to how to space the output. So it
doesn't matter how many spaces you type.

\item paragraphs are separated by one or more blank lines.

\item don't use the keyboard double quote character {\tt "}. Your
keyboard has single left quote {\tt '} and single right quote
{\tt '} keys. Reported speech is usually surrounded by double
quote marks ''thus''. Reported speech within reported speech, and
the first novel use of a technical term is usually surrounded by
single quotes: ''He said 'don't quote me on that'\,''.

\item \TeX\ breaks lines by looking for interword spaces and
sometimes by hyphenating. You can make an unbreakable interword
space with a {\em tie} which is written {\tt\~{}} ensuring that
the Mr in Mr~Smith is never orphaned. You can disable line
breaking altogether (including hyphenation) by putting text in a
box which \mbox{will simply hang out into the margin.}

\item You have already seen examples of {\em emphasized words}
typeset in italic. {\em Emphasis {\em within} emphasis is shown
in {\em Roman} type. But don't overdo it.}\/\footnote{This is a
footnote to the emphasized text. Note the use of an italic
correction to place the footnote mark correctly.}
\end{itemize}
```

- although your keyboard probably has only one kind of dash, typeset text requires four different kinds: the intra-word hyphen; a dash for numeric ranges (17–25); a punctuation dash—which should not have spaces round it—and the mathematical minus sign $(17 - 25)$.

- these keyboard characters are already reserved by LaTeX and need special treatment

$$\# \ \$ \ \% \ \& \ \backslash \ \{ \ \} \ \_ \ \char"5E \ \char"7E$$

3   Displays

The bulleted list in the previous section is one kind of *display*. You can make numbered lists

1. first item

   - and you can nest lists of different kinds
   ◇ as well as override the default tick mark

2. second item

Quotations may also be displayed by using indented paragraphs

   'Paragraph indentation is suppressed for short quotations'

There is another quotation environment for multiparagraph quotes.

   Longer quotations (those with more than one paragraph) use extra indentation ...
   ... at the start of paragraphs.

4   Type styles and sizes

By default, LaTeX sets type in a font called 'roman'. There are seven type styles that may be used with ordinary text—roman, **bold**, sans serif, *slanted*, SMALL CAPS and `typewriter`.

   You can have tiny, scriptsize, footnotesize, small, normalsize, large, Large, LARGE, huge and Huge text.

```
\begin{itemize}
\item although your keyboard probably has only one kind of dash,
typeset text requires four different kinds: the intra-word
hyphen; a dash for numeric ranges (17--25); a punctuation
dash---which should not have spaces round it---and the
mathematical minus sign ($17-25$).

\item these keyboard characters are already reserved by \LaTeX\
and need special treatment

\begin{center}
\# \$ \% \& $\backslash$ \{ \} \_ \^\ \~\
\end{center}
\end{itemize}

\section{Displays}

The bulleted list in the previous section is one kind of {\em
display}. You can make numbered lists \begin{enumerate} \item
first item \begin{itemize} \item and you can nest lists of
different kinds \item[$\diamond$] as well as override the default
tick mark \end{itemize} \item second item \end{enumerate}
Quotations may also be displayed by using indented paragraphs
\begin{quote} 'Paragraph indentation is suppressed for short
quotations' \end{quote} There is another  quotation environment
for multiparagraph quotes. \begin{quotation} Longer quotations
(those with more than one paragraph) use extra indentation \ldots

\ldots at the start of paragraphs.

\end{quotation}
\section{Type styles and sizes}

By default, \LaTeX\ sets type in a font called 'roman'. There are
seven type styles that may be used with ordinary text---roman,
{\bf bold}, {\sf sans serif}, {\sl slanted}, {\sc small caps} and
{\tt typewriter}.

You can have {\tiny tiny}, {\scriptsize scriptsize},
{\footnotesize footnotesize}, {\small small}, normalsize, {\large
large},  {\Large Large}, {\LARGE LARGE}, {\huge huge} and  {\Huge
Huge} text.
```

5   Mathematics

Mathematical formulae can be in-text like $x = \sum_{i=1}^{15} y_i/y_{i+1}$ or displayed

$$x = \sum_{i=1}^{15} \frac{y_i}{y_{i+1}}$$

and the position of subscripts and superscripts will be tweaked as necessary. This example shows the use of subscripts, superscripts and fractions. There are other commands for building matrices and large brackets.

TeX knows about dozens of maths symbols. Here are just a few

$$\aleph \quad \Re \quad \Im \quad \mho \quad \hbar \quad \wp \quad \imath \quad \jmath \quad \ell \quad \nabla \quad \partial \quad \surd \quad \forall \quad \exists \quad \neg \quad \backslash$$
$$\top \quad \bot \quad \| \quad \angle \quad \clubsuit \quad \diamondsuit \quad \heartsuit \quad \spadesuit \quad \prime \quad \emptyset \quad \infty \quad \mid \quad \flat \quad \natural \quad \sharp$$

6   Figures, tables and pictures

LaTeX has an easy to use table construction command. The table of maths commands above is an example of its use. You can make tables *float* which means that they will move to the top or bottom of a page of a page. The `table` and `figure` environments make floats and allow captions to be entered automatically into a list of figures or tables.

Finally, you can draw simple pictures like this

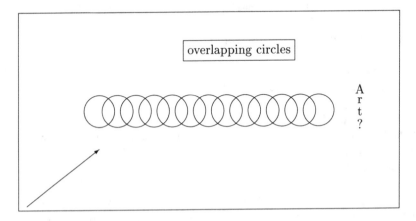

```
\section{Mathematics}

Mathematical formulae can be in-text  like $x=\sum^{15}_{i=1}
y_i/y_{i+1}$ or displayed \[ x=\sum^{15}_{i=1}
{{y_i}\over{y_{i+1}}}\] and the position of subscripts and
superscripts will be tweaked as necessary. This example shows the
use of subscripts, superscripts and fractions. There are other
commands for building matrices and large brackets.

\TeX\ knows about dozens of maths symbols. Here are just a few

\begin{center}\begin{tabular}{*{16}{c}}

$\aleph$ & $\Re$ & $\Im$ & $\mho$ & $\hbar$ & $\wp$ & $\imath$ &
$\jmath$ &  $\ell$ & $\nabla$ & $\partial$ & $\surd$ & $\forall$
& $\exists$ &  $\neg$ & $\backslash$\\
$\top$ & $\bot$ & $\|$ & $\angle$ & $\clubsuit$ & $\diamondsuit$
&  $\heartsuit$ &  $\spadesuit$ & $\prime$ & $\emptyset$ &
$\infty$ & $\vert$ & $\flat$ & $\natural$ & $\sharp$\\
\end{tabular}\end{center}
\section{Figures, tables and pictures}

\LaTeX\ has an easy to use table construction command. The table
of maths commands above is an example of its use. You can make
tables {\em float} which means that they will move to the top or
bottom of a page of a page. The {\tt table} and {\tt figure}
environments make floats and allow captions to be entered
automatically into a list of figures or tables.

Finally, you can draw simple pictures like this
\vspace*{1ex}
\begin{center}
\setlength{\unitlength}{1mm}
\fbox{
\begin{picture}(100,50)
\multiput(20,25)(5,0){13}{\circle{8}}
\put(43,40){\framebox{overlapping circles}}
\put(90,20){\shortstack{A\\r\\t\\?}}
\put(0,0){\vector(4,3){20}}
\end{picture}
}
\end{center}
```

2

Commands and variables

LaTeX is a programming language, with commands, variables and control structures. Fortunately, most of the time it is not necessary to actually program LaTeX, it being sufficient to use the predefined LaTeX commands. Full blown programming is described in Chapters 11 and 12: in this chapter the basics of LaTeX syntax are set down.

2.1 How to spot a command

A LaTeX source file contains mainly straight text interspersed with control sequences. Whenever a blank line is encountered, LaTeX starts a new paragraph. Apart from that, and the ten special control characters listed below, all control sequences begin with a backslash (\) character.

Some LaTeX commands directly produce typeset text or space, such as the sequence \LaTeX which produces the LaTeX logo. Many other sequences are *declarations* which affect the way formatting proceeds without directly producing any output text, for example \bf which causes type to be set in a **bold** font. LaTeX also maintains a set of named variables which hold the value of *counters* such as the current page number, *length* parameters such as \textwidth, the width of the text body on a page, and *boxes* which can hold typeset material such as a word or a whole page.

2.1.1 Special characters

There are ten special characters used in both plain TeX and LaTeX, and you must be careful not to let these slip through when typing text. They are

$$ \backslash \quad \% \quad \{ \quad \} \quad \# \quad \$ \quad \hat{} \quad \_ \quad \& \quad \~{} $$

Several of these characters are rather common in typed text, especially % and &. If you have to format text that has been prepared for another purpose, or by a typist who is unaware of TeX's idiosyncrasies, then it is worth doing a search and replace for these characters using your editor.

You should replace all occurrences of % with \% and likewise for each of the other characters, so that you get an ampersand & in the typeset output by typing \&. The only exception to this is the \ character which is generated by $\backslash$.

Be warned that the \\ command generates a line end, not a backslash! The ten special characters have the following meanings:

\ is the *escape* character and is used to introduce command symbols and words.

% is the*comment* character. It causes the rest of the line to be discarded.

{ and } are used to define *groups*, which will be discussed in the next section.

is the *macro parameter* character. Its use is described in Chapter 10.

$ is the *maths mode* character. LaTeX has two main modes — text mode for normal written paragraphs and mathematics mode for typesetting formulae. When LaTeX starts, it is in text mode. When it encounters a $ character, LaTeX switches to mathematics mode until it encounters another $, when it toggles back to text mode. (Just looking for the $ signs in a TeX file will not be sufficient to tell you when TeX is going in and out of maths mode because there are several other ways of performing this switch-over.)

^ and _ are single character commands that cause the immediately following text to be typeset as superscripts and subscripts accordingly. Their use is described in section 8.2.

& is used as a tabulation character

~ is a *tie*. It is treated just like a space character except that LaTeX will not break a line at a tie. You should get into the habit of using ties between words that should not be separated instead of spaces. In particular, always put a tie between a title and a name, as in `Mr~Smith`.

2.1.2   Groups

Often it is convenient to group blocks of text together as a single unit. Braces (the { and } characters) are used to delimit such blocks, and the result is called a *group*.

Groups have two main uses. Firstly, many LaTeX commands operate on the next 'thing' in the text. For instance the command `\underline Apple` produces A̲pple because the capital A is the next thing after the command. It would be tedious to underline a whole word by prefacing each character with an `\underline` command, but if you put braces around Apple then the whole word becomes a group and is used as the next 'thing' in sequence, hence `\underline{Apple}` produces A̲p̲p̲l̲e̲.

The second use of groups is to control the extent of declarations. Any declarations or changes to variables that are made inside a group are forgotten at the end of the group, and the original conditions restored. Technically, the *scope* of a declaration is local to the group in which it is declared[1]. In this example there are three nested groups, and at the beginning of each group a new typeface is selected. The old type face is automatically reselected as a group is exited.

    {\bf bold {\em emphasised {\rm roman text} text} text}
    produces
    bold *emphasised* roman text *text* **text**

---

[1]Actually there are a few variables that are *global*, such as the current page number, and their values are not restored at the end of a group.

2.1.3   Characters that are sometimes special

Immediately after some commands the three characters *, [and (are *sometimes* significant, although away from commands they produce the expected output. For instance, in the long example you will see that the command \subsection* generates a subsection heading without the number that would be printed using a \subsection command. If you need to follow a command with one of these characters then insert an empty group {} immediately after the command.

2.1.4   Control words and control symbols

The escape character \ introduces control sequences. These come in two kinds

⋄ *control words* made up of the letters A..Z and a..z. TₑX is case sensitive, so \xyz is not the same command as \xYz.

⋄ *control symbols* comprising a *single* non-alphabetic character

A control word is not allowed to have numbers in it, so \mycommand1 is read as the command \mycommand followed by the character 1. Where a number is needed as part of a command name, use roman numerals to give \mycommandi, \mycommandii and so on.

Confusion over the rules governing space after control words and symbols often gives rise to unexpected whitespace in TₑX output. When TₑX reads a control *word* it throws away all following whitespace and starts processing again at the next non-space character. If this was not done it would be impossible to typeset **abc** (using {\bf a\rm b\bf c}) because the spaces needed to terminate the commands would get into the output, producing **a** b **c**. On the other hand, since control *symbols* are known to be single characters TₑX does not consume space after a symbol, so \% \% gives % % not %%. If you *want* space to appear immediately after a control word use the command \␣ (a \ character followed by a space).

2.1.5   Keywords

TₑX also recognises a small number of keywords after certain commands. The complete list includes

⋄ The dimensional units bp, cc, cm, dd, em, ex, in, mm, pc, pt, sp, mu and true (section 11.3.2).

⋄ The special skip values fil, fill and ffill (section 11.4.2).

⋄ The skip modifiers plus and minus (section 11.4).

⋄ The font modifiers at and scaled (section 5.4.1).

⋄ Arithmetic keywords by and = (section 11.2.4).

⋄ Box modifiers width, depth, height, to and spread.

It is important to remember that these words do not normally mean anything to LATEX. If you type mm in normal text it will be printed as mm. It is only when LATEX is expecting a dimension and has already read a number that it will interpret mm as a keyword. That is why it does not matter that you do not at this stage know the meaning of the TEX keywords — the chances of you accidentally typing them in the relevant context are negligible.

2.1.6   Parameters

Some LATEX commands take parameters. The \underline{*text*} command is one such case — it always takes a single parameter. Some commands take more than one parameter, for instance \frac{a}{b} produces the fraction $\frac{a}{b}$.

There are commands which have optional parameters which are delimited using the [and] brackets. For instance in maths mode \sqrt{x} gives simply $\sqrt{x}$. Adding an optional argument gives a general root so \sqrt[n]{x} produces $\sqrt[n]{x}$.

A very few commands used for drawing pictures take coordinate parameters delimited by parentheses (and). As for the [and * characters, LATEX only checks for (characters *immediately* after a control word, so there must be no spaces between the parameters and the command.

2.2   Using commands inside parameters

Usually, as soon as LATEX encounters a command it replaces it with its definition, and continues this expansion process until a string of primitives is left, which are then executed. However, there are times when the point in your document file at which a command is written does not correspond to the point at which it is used. An example is a command to change the contents of the page header. The changes requested by the command will not actually be used until the next page is output. Note that the sectioning commands such as \chapter and \section fall into this category because they can be used to update the page header.

Very occasionally, it is necessary to tell LATEX to expand a command in a special way when it appears in the parameter to another command that might be used again later. There is a command \protect that may be placed in front of any other command to warn LATEX that it may be used in this deferred way.

In fact, the vast majority of LATEX users go through life without ever needing to use a \protect command (there are only 2 in the LATEX code for this book, for instance) so I suggest that you wait until you have an incomprehensible error message and then try \protecting the commands inside the parameter that is causing the problem.

For those that want the whole story, the commands that may cause problems are: any command that writes to an external file, such as the table of contents file or the commands to write to the terminal; any command that affects the page heading; any title page footnotes generated with \thanks and any command appearing in the parameter to an @-expression in an **array** or **tabular** environment (see page 70). A safe, although conservative, strategy is to place a \protect command before every command in the parameters to these commands except for length or counter commands.

2.3 Commands, declarations and environments

Simple commands such as `\LaTeX` just output text — in this case the LaTeX logo. There is a large set of text-generating commands that access characters that do not appear on the keyboard, such as `\alpha` α, `\sharp` $\sharp$ and `\heartsuit` $\heartsuit$. Chapter 5 contains tables describing these commands. Another simple text generating command is `\today`, which typesets the date current at the time the document was processed[2].

However, not all command sequences directly affect the output. The typesetting process is controlled by many *style parameters*, which select font type and size, page size, paragraph spacing and so on. Many control sequences modify these parameters without directly producing text output. For instance `\bf` selects a new font, but prints nothing. Such commands are called declarations. Some declarations such as the page width and height should be made at the beginning and remain in force throughout the document. These declarations are usually made in the preamble, i.e. before the `\begin{document}` command. Most declarations are local to their group, and their effects will be forgotten at the end of the group when the old values are restored.

An *environment* is a sort of super-group delimited by commands of the form

`\begin{`*environment-name*`}` *environment-text* `\end{`*environment-name*`}`

The `\begin{`*environment-name*`}` and the `\end{`*environment-name*`}` expand into a set of declarations and commands that make wholesale temporary changes to the current style. *environment-text* can be any chunk of LaTeX text which may itself contain environments so, like groups, environments may be nested. It is possible to define your own environments using the commands described in Chapter 10. Environments also define a new scope region, so any declarations made within *environment-text* will be reset after the `\end{`*environment-name*`}` command.

Of course, every document must have at least one environment: the `document` environment delimited by `\begin{document}` ... `\end{document}`.

2.4 LaTeX variables

LaTeX keeps track of six different kinds of variables, which will be discussed in some detail in Chapter 11. Each kind of variable is capable of storing information about a different kind of information. You can declare *registers* to hold these different kinds of data. The six kinds of register are

---

[2]This footnote contains a `\today` command from which you can see that the final copy for this book was produced on July 9, 1992.

1. *counters*, which hold integers in the range -2147483647 to $+2147483647$. The present page number, and the section number are held in counters, so you will understand that TEX can not easily typeset books that have more than 2,147,483,647 pages. This is not much of a restriction — a typical 1000 page computer manual on my shelf is 4cm thick, so the smallest book that TEX could not handle would be more than 85km thick.

2. *lengths*, which hold distance measurements. There is a length register called `\textwidth` that defines the width of the text body on the page.

3. *boxes*, which hold rectangular pieces of typeset text. The most important property of a box is that it is *indivisible*, so once some typeset words have been put together in a box they cannot be broken up[3]. A common use of boxes is therefore to override TEX's hyphenation algorithm. A word put in a box is unbreakable because boxes are indivisible. The second page of the large example shows an example of text which has been boxed, and TEX gave up trying to find a good line break and simply let it hang out into the right margin. TEX uses two kinds of boxes to build pages. A horizontal box (or *hbox* for short) is a one dimensional box that can only extend horizontally. Loosely speaking, an hbox corresponds to a line of text. Unless you tell TEX not to, it will break hboxes up into units about the width of a page, and then stack them into vertical boxes (*vboxes*, or *parboxes*) which have depth as well as width.

4. *token lists*, which hold strings of TEX commands. These are used internally for special effects. For instance, there is a token list called `\everypar` which holds a string of commands that are executed every time TEX starts a new paragraph. Some legalistic documents require every paragraph to be numbered, and by adding numbering commands to the `\everypar` token list you could get this effect automatically without having to explicitly number the individual paragraphs.

5. *skip registers*, which hold inter-word and inter-line spaces. In TEX these spaces are flexible in size and can shrink or expand as necessary to ensure even spacing. In fact their operation is rather like little springs placed between the words which act like rigid units. Each spring has a *natural length* which is its preferred size, a shrinkability and a stretchability. In extreme cases, TEX will expand springs more than is allowed by these values, but a warning message will be issued.

6. *maths skip registers*. The spacing rules in maths mode are quite different to the normal rules of typesetting, and so a special kind of spring is used.

A full discussion of these variables and how to manipulate them is deferred to Chapter 11, although you will find occasional references to LATEX's style parameters in the intervening chapters.

---

[3]This is not strictly true since TEX does have an unboxing command.

3

Document styles

Document styles differentiate the look of one document from another. In essence a style is a *template* into which your text will be fitted. The style defines fonts, section headings, running titles and so on. Every document must have exactly one parent style, but subsidiary style files may be read in to produce minor variations.

LaTeX provides four standard styles `article`, `report`, `book` and `letter`, but the 'look' of all these styles is similar. The long example in Chapter 1 shows the basic layout — default type size of 10pt, arabic page numbers in the footer, titles in large bold font and so on. The `letter` style is rather different and will be described in section 3.3, but `article`, `report` and `book` are closely related, the main differences being:

◇ `article` runs the title, abstract and text without page breaks. `report` and `book` use separate pages for the title and the abstract.

◇ `article` does not support chapters.

◇ `book` prints double sided pages by default and has a `\part` command for breaking a long document into different parts.

The main style is specified as a parameter to the `\documentstyle` command which should be the first command in a LaTeX file. An optional parameter to `\documentstyle` can be used to specify a comma separated list of subsidiary styles to be read in when LaTeX starts. This book was formatted using the standard `book` style file, but I created a subsidiary style called `eh` which modifies the definitions of section headings and page sizes to suit the Ellis Horwood house style. This book has an index, so I also called up the `makeidx` style to define some useful commands for index making. The first line of the source file is therefore

```
\documentstyle[eh,makeidx]{book}
```

3.1 How to find style files

Style files have names of the form *style*.sty and contain closely packed TeX commands. Because they have to be read every time they are called in it is normal practice to remove all the comments from a style file and as much white space as possible. Naturally this makes them difficult to read, so usually a parallel file called *style*.doc is kept with the original comments[1].

---

[1] In fact even .doc files can be difficult to read, but see Chapter 12.

3.1.1   The inputs directory

Every TEX system has a reserved directory called the *inputs* directory where style files are kept. Typically it will be something like `/usr/local/lib/tex/inputs` on Unix, `\tex\inputs` on MS-DOS or `TEX$DISK:[TEX.INPUTS]` on VMS. TEX automatically looks in this directory whenever it needs to read something in. Usually it looks in the directory it was started from first, so you can also keep your own style files locally, without disrupting the main system styles.

It is a good idea to list all the `.sty` files in your inputs directory so that you get an idea of what styles are available to you. At the very least you should see `book.sty`, `article.sty`, `report.sty` and `letter.sty`. You should also see files with names like `bk10.sty`, `bk11.sty` and `bk12.sty` which are subsidiary styles for book that define a range of font selection commands based on 10, 11 and 12pt type respectively. If you cannot find these files then you are either looking in the wrong place, or there is something seriously wrong with your LATEX installation.

Not all style files actually adjust the style. Many styles add extra commands to LATEX. For instance the `bezier` style which you will find in your inputs directory adds commands to plot curves by typesetting a series of overlapping full stops. Some of these 'extra' commands will be described in the main part of this book and you will be warned if you need to read in an extra style file. In Chapter 13 some useful style files that are not presently part of the standard distribution will be described, along with advice on how to obtain them.

3.2   Standard subsidiary style files

A variety of standard subsidiary styles are supplied with every LATEX system. Usually, you access these styles by putting their name in the optional parameter to the `\documentstyle` command as shown above. The exceptions are the font size selection options. By default, all the standard styles use 10pt characters as their base size. The style options `11pt` and `12pt` override the default to select 11pt and 12pt characters. When these styles are found in the optional parameter, a file of the form *abrv*`11.sty` is read in where *abrv* is `bk` for book, `rep` for `report` and `art` for `article`. The standard subsidiary styles are summarised below. There may well be other styles available to you, and you should ask for a copy of the documentation or read the associated `.doc` file for further information.

`11pt` use 11pt type as default.

`12pt` use 12pt type as default.

`draft` insert a black bar at the end of any line that overhangs into the right margin.

`twoside` change margins for double sided printing (default in `book`).

`twocolumn` use twocolumn printing as default.

`titlepage` makes `article` use `report` style abstract and titlepage conventions, with each on a separate page.

`openbib` produce open style bibliographies.

`leqno` put equation numbers on the left.

`fleqn` left align displayed mathematical formulae.

`ifthen` define the program control commands described in section 12.4.10.

`bezier` define the `\bezier` curve drawing command described in section 7.5.8.

3.3 Letters

The `letter` standard style provides a set of special commands that are not available with the other standard styles. Many of the commands described elsewhere in this book are unavailable in `letter` style, such as the sectioning and table of contents commands.

A single LaTeX source file can contain many letters, each defined within a `letter` environment. An example letter, and its corresponding output is shown in Figures 3.1 and 3.2.

At the top of the file (usually before the `\begin{document}`) you must specify your standard signature and address using the commands `\signature{text}` and `\address{text}`. and these will be automatically inserted in each letter. You can also insert a `\makelabels` command which will generate a sheet of address labels, one for each letter in the file.

Each letter is enclosed by

> `\begin{letter}{addressee}` ... `\end{letter}`.

addressee contains the name and address of the recipient and will be used for the address label and at the top left of the printed letter. You can use `\\` commands to start new lines within the *addressee* text.

The `\opening{salutation}` command prints the *salutation* on a line of its own with suitable vertical spacing and is used to start the letter text. Some LaTeX installations have special letter styles that incorporate headed note paper. Usually the heading is generated by the `\opening` command, so do not leave it out even if you want a blank salutation.

The `\closing{valediction}` command prints *valediction* on a line of its own and then appends your signature, leaving a space for you to sign your name.

After the `\closing` command you can use `\ps{text}`, `\cc{text}`, `\encl{text}` to add a postscript, a list of other recipients (carbon copies) and a list of enclosures.

3.4 Page layout

A LaTeX page is made up of the *body*, a *header*, a *footer* and left and right margins as shown in Figure 3.3. The body is where the main part of the text goes, and it may have one or two columns (Chapter 13 describes a style file that allows you to have as many columns as you like, but this is not part of the standard LaTeX system.) The sizes of these regions are defined by a set of LaTeX size parameters. By

Department of Computer Science
Royal Holloway, University of London
Egham Hill
Egham
Surrey
TW20 0EX
ENGLAND

June 1992

Santa Claus
3, The Fairy Grotto
North Pole

Dear Sir,

Enclosed one Christmas present list, nicely typeset using LATEX. The presents are in priority order: I would particularly like a new workstation, as I've had the last one for three months and it is now obsolete. Hope you and the reindeer are well.

Yours sincerely,

Adrian Johnstone
Email: `adrian@cs.rhbnc.ac.uk`

Last year's list seemed to go astray judging by the rather poor response. This year I have sent a copy to the Chief Elf just to make sure.

cc: Head of Elf workshop

encl: Present list

Figure 3.1 An example typeset letter

```
\documentstyle{letter}
%
\signature{Adrian Johnstone\\
Email: {\tt adrian@cs.rhbnc.ac.uk}}
%
\address{Department of Computer Science\\
Royal Holloway, University of London\\Egham
Hill\\Egham\\Surrey\\TW20 0EX\\\sc England}
%
% These three commands do nothing in the standard style
%
\name{Dr A Johnstone}                      % return name
\telephone{}                               % sender's telephone number
\location{Department of Computer Science} %sender's department
%
\makelabels  % make an address label
\begin{document}
\begin{letter}{Santa Claus\\
3, The Fairy Grotto\\
North Pole
}
\opening{Dear Sir,}
Enclosed one Christmas present list, nicely typeset using \LaTeX.
The presents are in priority order: I would particularly like a
new workstation, as I've had the last one for three months and it
is now obsolete. Hope you and the reindeer are well.
\closing{Yours sincerely,}
\ps{Last year's list seemed to go astray judging by the rather
poor response. This year I have sent a copy to the Chief Elf just
to make sure.}                 %postscript
\cc{Head of Elf workshop}  %carbon copy
\encl{Present list}        %enclosure
\end{letter}
%
% You can put more letter environments here
%
\end{document}
```

Figure 3.2 Source code for letter

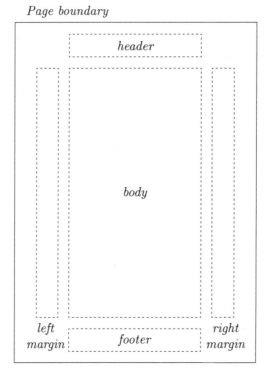

Figure 3.3 LaTeX page structure

default, TeX will produce output for American sized 8.5 × 11 inch paper with one inch margins. If you are a European LaTeX user this will probably be unsatisfactory since A4 standard paper is considerably larger. You will find a full discussion of how to change page layout in Chapter 11. For now, ask another user if your system provides a style file called `A4.sty`. If it does not, try adding the lines shown in Figure 3.4 to the start of your file before the `\begin{document}` command.

3.4.1   Single and double column printing

By default, text is set in a single column the same width as the page body. LaTeX will switch into two column typesetting if you issue a `\twocolumn` command or if you use the `[twocolumn]` style option in which case LaTeX will start typesetting the document in two column mode. The complementary `\onecolumn` command restores single column printing. Both of these commands cause the preceding text to be output and a new page to be started.

In two column mode floats and footnotes will also be restricted to columns. You can get a full page width banner over a two column page by using an optional argument to `\twocolumn`:

```
% quick and dirty A4 page sizes for LaTeX
\oddsidemargin=0mm\evensidemargin=0mm
\textwidth=149mm\textheight=237mm
\topmargin=-45pt\headheight=12truept\headsep=25pt
\footskip=37pt\footheight=12pt
\hoffset=5mm\voffset=8mm
```

Figure 3.4 A4 page size commands

style	examples		
arabic	1	2	10
roman	i	ii	x
Roman	I	II	X
alph	a	b	j
Alph	A	B	J

Table 3.1 Page numbering styles

$\qquad$ \twocolumn[*full-width text*]

will start a new page and then typeset the *full-width text* at the top before setting the succeeding text in two-column mode.

3.4.2   Vertical page alignment

When typesetting books the vertical spacing is usually adjusted so that full page bodies are exactly the same length. In articles and other less formal documents it is usual to leave the page body at its natural length. The commands \flushbottom and \raggedbottom enable and disable adjustment of vertical spacing. The default in the book style and when the [twoside] document style option is in use is \flushbottom.

3.4.3   Page numbering

By default, the page number will appear centred in the footer printed as an arabic number. The \pagenumbering{*numberstyle*} command sets the printing style for page numbers. *numberstyle* can be one of the styles shown in Table 3.1. Usually, roman is used for the page numbers in the table of contents and other top matter such as the preface, and arabic numbering is used in the main document.

3.4.4   Changing the header and footer

The contents of the header and footer are specified by the *page style*. The command \pagestyle{*style*} changes the pagestyle for pages including the one containing the \pagestyle command and subsequent pages to *style*. \thispagestyle{*style*}

style	header	footer
plain	empty	centred page number
empty	empty	empty
headings	defined by document style	empty
myheadings	defined by \markboth and \markright commands	empty

Table 3.2 Page styles for modifying headers and footers

makes a temporary change to the style for the page containing the \thispagestyle command only.

The four predefined page styles are listed in Table 3.2. If you want other combinations, such as running titles in the footer you will have to learn how to write your own style files, a subject treated in Chapter 12.

The headings page style causes the standard styles to generate a running header comprising the sectional unit name and (in books) the chapter name typeset in italic capitals, along with the page number.

The default action of the myheadings style is the same as for the headings style, but you can specify your own headings using the \markboth{*right*}{*left*} and \markright{*right*} commands.

If you are using the twoside document option (the default in book style) then the *right* argument specifies the header for odd numbered pages and the *left* argument for even numbered pages. Documents prepared for single sided printing use only the *right* heading. The first page of a document will be typeset with an empty page, but you can use the titlepage environment to make an empty titlepage, after which the 'real' first page will have a header. Chapters are also set with an empty header on their first page.

The \mark... commands may require \protect commands in front of commands used in their parameters.

There is a bug in LaTeX that causes the \pagestyle{empty} command to misbehave when used in a document with the \maketitle command described on page 33. If your first page has a number on, try putting the pagestyle{empty} command immediately after the \maketitle command.

3.5   How TeX builds pages

Characters, lines, paragraphs and pages are the basic units with which LaTeX deals. All of these object fit into rectangular boxes of different sizes, and TeX spends most of its time simply fitting boxes together into larger and larger boxes.

As TeX reads the source file it breaks lines up into words separated by whitespace. Whitespace is a string of one or more space, tab or newline characters, except that a completely blank line marks the end of a paragraph. The actual amount of space between words is ignored — a single space character means the same as ten to TeX.

TEX continues stringing these words together on one long line separated by space markers until it has read an entire paragraph. It then adds indentation at the beginning of the paragraph and chops the line up into segments roughly as wide as the printed page. It does this first by attempting to break the line at a space. If no suitable break can be found LATEX applies American hyphenation rules to try and find a line break in the middle of a word[2].

When the linebreaks have been set the lines are *justified* by stretching or shrinking the interword space until all the lines are the same length. Each line is then put into an hbox and subsequently is treated as an indivisible unit. The boxes are stacked, separated by the interline space into a paragraph which is then put into a vbox.

Parboxes for successive paragraphs are then stacked together, separated by the interparagraph space, to make a page. When enough have accumulated, TEX looks for a page break and then, if the \flushbottom declaration is in effect, it stretches or shrinks the interline and interparagraph space until all the pages are the same vertical height. The headline and footline are then added (usually containing at least the page number) and the page is then written on the output file.

Although TEX's automatic line and page breaking algorithms usually produce beautiful results, there are occasions when manual intervention is required.

3.6   Controlling line breaking

The \\ command and its synonym \newline force a linebreak without justification leaving a ragged right. The *-form * inhibits page breaking immediately after the line. Both commands take an optional length argument which adds extra interline space after the line, so that \\[2ex] leaves a double space before the next line.

By default LATEX will leave words hanging out into the right margin if it is unable to find a good line break. A warning message beginning Overfull \hbox ... will be printed. The \sloppy declaration will produce lines that have too much space in them rather than overhanging, in which case an Underfull \hbox ... warning will be given. The default operation can be restored with the \fussy declaration. The sloppypar environment will typeset complete paragraphs in sloppy mode.

You can give hints to the line breaking algorithm with \linebreak[*digit*] which encourages linebreaking at that point and \nolinebreak[*digit*] which discourages linebreaking. The *digit* argument may take a value from 0 to 4 — if it is absent then the default value of 4 is used. The larger the value the more strongly the operation is encouraged. A value of 4 forces or completely avoids a line break. (Hence \nolinebreak has the same effect as inserting a tie).

The paragraph indentation is inhibited if a \noindent command is the first thing in the paragraph. A paragraph indent can be forced with an \indent where it would otherwise be suppressed.

---

[2]English hyphenation rules are rather more strict, so to British eyes TEX has a tendency to over-hyphenate, but most people are unaware of the difference

3.7   Controlling hyphenation

TEX's hyphenation algorithm is one of its strengths, and it should rarely be necessary to intervene. However, TEX may occasionally fail to hyphenate an unusual compound word, and it may over-hyphenate if the text is being set in narrow columns.

Hyphenation of a word may be disabled by putting it into a box, after which it is treated as an indivisible unit by the line breaking algorithm. There are many box making commands described in Chapter 11, but the simplest way to make an indivisible box is with the command \mbox{*text*}. The *text* will be typeset as a single unit, so the single word \mbox{*antidisestablishmentarialism*} will not be hyphenated, but is likely to lead to Overfull \hbox ... errors!

The discretionary hyphen command \- may be used to show the places in a word where hyphenation is allowed. It is used if TEX is failing to detect a valid hyphenation point, which may happen if you use unusual compound words such as chemical names. A word containing discretionary hyphens will *only* be hyphenated at the discretionary points. It is also the case that TEX will not hyphenate words that have control sequences such as accents embedded in them, or words that are typeset using the \tt font.

\hyphenation{*words*} adds new word patterns to TEX's hyphenation rules. *words* is a list of words separated by spaces with each hyphenation point indicated by a -. Be sure to include all reasonable hyphenations otherwise you may find that sometimes when you use the word it generates a bad line break.

3.8   Controlling page breaking

A vertical break is forced with a \newpage command. If two column text is being set then \newpage starts a new column. \clearpage always starts a new page, leaving a blank column if necessary. I make a point of always using \clearpage to start a new page, because you can get a surprise if you use \newpage and then later on decide to switch to two column printing.

\cleardoublepage forces a start on a new odd-numbered page, leaving a blank page if necessary. The \chapter command uses \cleardoublepage to ensure that chapters start on a right-hand page. Multiple consecutive \clearpage or \newpage commands will only cause a single page break. To get a series of blank pages you must separate the page throw commands with some invisible text such as a ~ character.

The page breaking algorithm may be given hints with the \pagebreak[*digit*] and \nopagebreak[*digit*] commands which work just like the \linebreak and \nolinebreak commands described in the section 3.6.

The \samepage declaration disables page breaking altogether except where explicitly permitted by \pagebreak or \nopagebreak commands. Use \samepage sparingly, and remember that it is a declaration, not a command like \nopagebreak, so you must enclose the region of text to be kept on one page in braces or LATEX will try and put the rest of your document on a single page.

4

Structuring a document

Punctuation is used within sentences and paragraphs to aid the reader by breaking up long strings of words into comprehensible phrases. Well written prose has a pleasing rhythm which is different from the colloquial, spoken word.

Technical documents need structure at a higher level as well. Literary works often rely for their effect on surprising the reader with unusual twists of language. Whilst textbooks and papers should not be full of clichés, successful presentation of technical details relies more on reinforcement of ideas than literary fireworks. You get the effect of reinforcement without repetition by structuring your document so that the reader has some idea about what is coming next. So use chapter titles, section headings and introductions to advertise topics in advance.

As well as helping readers as they go along, good section structure is vital for books that are to be used for reference. Ideally, your reader should be able to look at a table of contents and quickly home in on the part of the document that treats a particular topic.

It is possible to go overboard with nested subsections. Chapters, sections and subsections are usually more than enough for most documents. In this, as in most matters of style, base your work on other people's books and reports until you feel confident enough to break the rules. Legalistic documents, such as programming language definitions, sometimes justify deeper and more systematic structure, but this is at the expense of readability. Try reading a programming language standard like [ISO80, the ISO Pascal standard] and see if you agree.

4.1 The titlepage

LaTeX will automatically build a titlepage when you issue the \maketitle command. This would normally be the first thing in your source file following the \begin{document}. The exact form is specified by the style file: in book and report styles the title will be on a separate page but in article the title is inserted without page throws. The title and author will be set centred, with appropriate vertical spacing and font sizing. The titling commands are demonstrated in the large example at the end of Chapter 1.

Before issuing a \maketitle you must declare the title and the author, and optionally, the date.

\title{text} declares text to be the title. You can use font and size changing commands within the text parameter as well as forcing line breaks with \\

commands.

\author{*name1* \and *name2* \and ...} declares the authors separated by \and commands. The authors will be set in separate blocks of text side-by-side on the page.

\date{*text*} inserts *text* as the date. If there is no \date declaration then the current date is used. To suppress the date altogether, try \date{} (i.e. supply a null argument to the \date command).

The \thanks{*text*} command produces a footnote to the title page which is usually used for addresses, or to acknowledge funding.

4.1.1   Do-it-yourself titles

If you want complete control over the formatting of the titlepage then replace the \maketitle command with a titlepage environment. This produces a single page containing only the text specified within the environment (i.e. with blank headers and footers) and then resets the page counter to one. You can put any normal sequence of typesetting commands within the titlepage environment.

4.2   Abstracts

The abstract environment (available only in the article and report standard styles) sets the enclosed text indented with the word **Abstract** centred above. In a report, or an article with the [titlepage] option the abstract appears on a separate page. The large example in Chapter 1 shows the abstract environment in use.

4.3   Sectioning commands

LATEX provides a set of sectioning commands which generate section headings and, optionally, make entries in a table of contents and update the running header. The specific effect of these commands is defined in the style file, and not all commands are available in all styles. In particular, letter does not provide any sectioning commands at all. The seven standard commands are listed below. Note that sectioning commands should be nested according to the ordering here, the only exception being \part which is optional.

command	depth	
\part	-1	(0 in article)
\chapter	0	
\section	1	
\subsection	2	
\subsubsection	3	
\paragraph	4	
\subparagraph	5	

Each level of sectioning command has an associated counter which is initialised to zero every time the enclosing section number changes. By default, all sectioning commands increment and print the section number before the heading. The exact form of the section number is customisable in the style file, but the standard styles simply separate the separate levels with a period and print the numbers in arabic.

If the command is followed by a * then the printing *and incrementing* of the associated counter is suppressed. The table of contents entry and updating of the running header are also suppressed. This is useful for subsidiary subheadings and in documents such as a *Curriculum Vitae* where numbered headings would be too fussy.

4.4   Making a table of contents

Most chapter-oriented documents and long articles benefit from a table of contents to help the reader navigate around. The command \tableofcontents causes LaTeX to typeset a table of contents before continuing with your file. Normally this command would be found near the front of a document, after the title and abstract (if any).

When you use a normal sectioning command (i.e. not one of the *-forms) an entry is written on a separate output file with the same name as the main source file but with a file type of .toc. The information written to the toc file actually comprises LaTeX commands describing the table of contents pages, that will be read and executed the next time LaTeX processes the parent file. That is to say, if you have asked for table of contents generation, LaTeX looks to see if a toc file already exists and if so, processes it before continuing with the parent file. In any case it creates a new toc file and writes commands to it whilst processing the main file.

This is a technique that LaTeX uses extensively to carry information across runs. TeX is a one pass system that looks at each line of your source file in sequence, so it cannot in one operation scan your file and create a table of contents.

As a result, table of contents information (as well as cross referencing, bibliography, indexing, glossary, list of figures and list of tables records) is always at least one step behind. If you make a change to a LaTeX document that may alter the table of contents you will have to run LaTeX at least twice for the document to become self-consistent.

4.5   List of figures and list of tables

The \listoffigures and \listoftables commands work in the same way as \tableofcontents except that the entries are produced by \caption commands in table and figures (see section 7.3.3) rather than the sectioning commands as for the table of contents. The information is written on .lof and .lot files respectively.

4.6   Adding entries to contents or tables files

Sometimes it is helpful to add lines to one of these files. The most common example is when non-numbered sections are required with a table of contents (remember that the *-form suppresses table of contents information). The command

```
\addcontentsline{file}{level}{text}
```

adds an entry to *file* (which may be toc, lof or lot). *level* is used to specify the formatting of the entry and should be the name of one of the sectioning commands such as chapter. If *file* is lot then *level* must be table, if lof then *level* must be figure. *entry* forms the actual text, and corresponds to the parameter of a sectioning or caption command. If you use a very long entry for *text* you may overflow an internal buffer, causing TEX to report a TeX capacity exceeded error.

In the standard styles, contents entries comprise a section number and a section title set on the left. The indentation of the section number is controlled by *level*, and the number is set in a fixed size box. (You may find the space allowed for the section number inadequate for chapters with many subsections, in which case see Chapter 12.) To produce your own entries that align with those produced by the sectioning commands, use

```
\addcontentsline{file}{level}
{\protect{\numberline{section-number}{section-title}}}
```

4.7   Adding free text to contents or tables files

More general text (such as LATEX commands) can be added to a file using

```
\addtocontents{file}{text}
```

which simply writes *text* to the file specified as above. The text will be incorporated into the document on the next LATEX pass.

Remember that since both the \addcontentsline and \addtocontents commands write to an external file, some commands in *text* may need to be preceded with a \protect command.

4.8   Making appendices

The declaration \appendix changes the way the top level section of a document is numbered so that appendix sections are numbered alphabetically. \appendix also resets the section and chapter counters back to zero and changes the chapter unit name to Appendix. The effect of these changes is that after an \appendix declaration any \chapter commands in the book and report styles or \section commands in the article style will generate a heading of the form

Appendix A

and 'numbering' will continue from **A**.

4.9   Footnotes

A footnote is produced with the command \footnote[*number*]{*text*}. If the optional argument is present then the note is numbered using it, otherwise the `footnote` counter is stepped and used instead. The number representation is defined by the style file — in the standard styles arabic numerals are used.

Occasionally, a footnote will be requested so close to the bottom of a page that there is insufficient space to typeset it. In such a case, the footnote will automatically run on to the next page. There is a bug in LaTeX that means that if a page of floats, such as figures or table, appears on the page after a footnote begins, the continuation of the footnote will not appear until the next text page. This rare problem has to be fixed by reworking the text.

The `\footnote` command can only be used in normal text paragraphs — it cannot be used inside a box for instance. For these situations, two other commands are provided that allow 'simulation' of the normal footnote command.

> `\footnotemark[`*number*`]`
>
>> inserts a footnote mark in the text exactly as for the `\footnote` except that no actual footnote is produced.
>
> `\footnotetext[`*number*`]{`*text*`}`
>
>> produces a footnote just like `\footnote` except that no footnote mark is placed in the text.

4.10   Marginal notes

Marginal notes are similar to footnotes but are placed in the left or right margins, | *A note* | like the one next to this paragraph.

The command `\marginpar[`*lefttext*`]{`*righttext*`}` makes a marginal note. In `[doublesided]` documents the notes are placed in the *outside* margin — left for even numbered (left hand) pages and right for odd (right hand) pages. For single sided printing, marginal notes are placed on the right. If the optional argument is present and the note is created in the left margin, then *lefttext* will be used for the note, otherwise *righttext* will be used. By default, marginal notes are set in roman text: I produced the note above with `\marginpar{\fbox{\small\em A note}}`.

The declaration `\reversemarginpar` reverses the normal ordering, so that even page notes will appear on the right. `\normalmarginpar` restores the default behaviour.

The marginal note is placed so that it aligns vertically with the line containing the `\marginpar` command. If there is a clash, later notes will be moved down and a warning message will be issued. If you switch between the `\normalmarginpar` and `\reversemarginpar` modes whilst marginal notes are being output, shifting may fail, leaving notes overprinted.

4.11   Using multiple files

A long document takes a long time to process. Often it is convenient to split the source file up and process just one section at a time, until all the parts are satisfactory when they can be brought back together again. You can insert the contents of another file in your master file with the command `\input{`*filename*`}` which reads the text from *filename* before continuing with the parent file. If *filename* has no file type then .tex will be appended. If the file cannot be found then an error is issued and TEX prompts for another filename. (It is sometimes not possible to get out of this prompting loop. If you get stuck like this, try typing nul in response to the prompt and TEX will read in an empty file, effectively returning you to the main file.)

4.11.1   Selective inclusion of files

More sophisticated file handling is possible using the include commands. The individual files are called into the parent file using \include{*filename*} commands by analogy with \input. In the preamble, i.e. before the \begin{document} command, insert an \includeonly{*filename1,filename2,...*} command listing the files that you want processed on this run.

At each subsequent \include{*filename*}, LATEX looks to see if *filename* is in the list of files defined by the \includeonly command. If it is, then LATEX starts a new page, includes the file and then starts another new page. If *filename* is not found a warning message is issued and processing continues. If there is no \includeonly command then all files are included. Since included files are always surrounded by page breaks it is best to break the file at Chapter boundaries.

4.12   Writing a message during processing

Sometimes it is useful to type out messages to the user as a LATEX file is being processed. The command \typeout{*text*} simply prints out *text* on the terminal as LATEX is running. Commands in *text* are executed before being printed out, so the use of formatting commands such as \it should be avoided, since in general they will produce things that cannot be represented on a terminal. If you want to print out a command name then precede the command with the command \protect. Because LATEX will interpret *text* before printing it, a string of spaces in *text* will be replaced by a single space in the output. The command \space forces a single space to be printed, so a string of spaces can be obtained with a string of \space commands. The command \thepage prints out the page number, so to get LATEX to print

```
Present value printed by \thepage is      18
```

you could use

```
\typeout{Present value of \protect\thepage is
          \space\space\space\space\space \thepage}
```

4.13   Varying output during a run

It can also be useful to get the user to type information in that can be used to vary the output from a particular source file. A common requirement is to specify which parts of a long document are to be processed.

The command \typein[*commandname*]{*text*} prints *text* on the terminal as for \typeout. The same constraints on the form of *text* apply. LaTeX then waits for the user to type a line on the terminal before proceeding. If the optional argument is present, it must contain the name of a command (i.e. the first character must be a backslash \). The line typed by the user is assigned to that command without any interpretation and may be used subsequently to control the output. So the short file

```
\documentstyle{article}
\begin{document}
\typein[\myname]{What is your name? }
\typein[\mystyle]{How would you like it printed? }
\mystyle\myname
\end{document}
```

when processed by LaTeX produces the following dialogue:

```
What is your name?

\myname=Adrian
How would you like it printed?

\mystyle=\Large\bf
[1]
```

and typesets my name in large bold letters. If you just type a carriage return in response to the style command the \mystyle will be defined to be null, so the name will be printed in the default style.

4.14   Making an index

Every technical book should have an index, and there is no easy route to the construction of a thorough and useful one. LaTeX cannot help you decide which entries to include and how exactly to format them, but it will keep track of index entries and the pages they fall on for you using a mechanism similar to the table of contents construction commands. There is one important difference between a table of contents and an index, though, and that is that indices are usually sorted alphabetically, whereas a table of contents is invariably listed in page ascending order. This make the use of an auxiliary program almost mandatory for index construction because LaTeX only makes a single pass over the source file and has no facilities for sorting. This is fine for table of contents generation because the printed order is the same as the order in which the entries are generated, but obviously inadequate for an index.

The first piece of advice is to leave construction of the index until the rest of the document is finished. Then the boring task of subject selection can be performed in a single sitting. A good way to start deciding which subjects to place in the index is to get a list of all the words in your document in alphabetical order and strike out the ones that should definitely not be indexed, such as simple parts of speech. It is quite easy to write a program that replaces every space character in your document with a carriage return (a global search and replace using your text editor might suffice) and the operating system sort utility can then be used to put the words in ascending order and eliminate any duplicates. (If you are using MS-DOS you are likely to find that the MS-DOS sort command is inadequate because it can only handle files up to 64K byte in length. Many utility packages for MS-DOS provide a better sort command).

Having decided on a set of entries you must mark the places in the text that are to be indexed. Do not make the mistake of indexing every single occurrence of the word. You should index the places where the item is defined and discussed at length, not every cross reference. You may find that the same item is used in several contexts, and this may justify several separate index sub-entries. As in all such matters, have a look at the indices to books that you use and try to emulate their practice.

4.14.1   Writing an index file

The LaTeX index entries are collected on a file called *name*.idx by analogy with the .toc file used for table of contents entries. The entries are only written if there is a \makeindex command before the \begin{document}. LaTeX will run faster if index writing is suppressed by leaving out the \makeindex.

Wherever you want an index entry generated, add the command \index{*text*} immediately after the word to be indexed. If you leave a space before the \index command then a page break might intervene and generate an index entry that was one page off. Each \index writes a single line to the .idx file of the form \indexentry{*text*}{*pagenumber*} where *text* is the text from the \index command and *pagenumber* is the number of the page containing the \index command. As for table of contents generation, several LaTeX runs may be required to stabilise the page numbers.

These basic LaTeX commands are not sufficient to make a complete index for you. Naturally, LaTeX writes the .idx file in the order in which it finds the \indexentry commands, so at the very least you need to sort the .idx file to provide an alphabetically ordered index.

4.14.2   The theindex environment

At the end of your document you can use typeset the index by surrounding it with

```
\begin{theindex} ... \end{theindex}
```

This will typeset the word **Index** as for a chapter heading, and set double column formatting. Within a theindex environment, the commands \item, \subitem and \subsubitem are defined to start a new line with increasing amounts of indentation, and should be used to introduce each item in the index. The command \indexspace is intended to be used before the first item beginning with a new letter in the index, marking off the different alphabetical blocks. The exact form of the theindex environment is specified in the style file.

4.14.3   How to turn an index file into an index

The contents of the `.idx` file is not directly usable in the index. However, if you perform a `sort` on the index file, and then add the following commands to the end of your document then you can get a rough and ready index:

```
\begin{theindex}
\newcommand{\indexentry}[2]{\item #1, #2}
\input{myfile.idx}
\end{theindex}
```

(Of course, in the above `myfile.idx` should be replaced with the name of the sorted index file.) The `\newcommand` definition is explained in Chapter 10 — suffice to say here that it will take each line of the `.idx` file and typeset the indexed item followed by a comma and the page on which it occurs.

This cheap and cheerful index will need a good deal of tidying up. Firstly, an `\indexspace` command should be inserted between each alphabetical block. More importantly, multiple `\index` commands will appear as multiple adjacent index entries and you should rearrange them to show a single entry with a list of pages. Finally, real indices use hierarchy with sub-items refining the main entry.

There are several index making programs available that are designed to help build LaTeX indices. A popular one (`makeindex` or `makeindx` on MS-DOS systems) described in Chapter 13, will automatically perform the housekeeping tasks such as telescoping multiple entries. If you have such a program, use it rather than trying to do the job yourself.

4.15   Making a glossary

The declaration `\makeglossary` when it appears in the preamble switches on the creation of a glossary `.glo` file. The `\glossary{`*text*`}` command writes a line to the `.glo` file of the form `\glossaryentry{`*text*`}{`*pagenumber*`}`, just like the `\indexentry` command. You can use similar manual procedures to typeset the glossary, but there is no glossary environment or special set of glossary formatting commands.

4.16   Suppressing output files

The generation of the `.toc`, `.lof`, `.lot`, `.idx`, `.glo` and `.aux` files will be switched off if you put a `\nofiles` command in the preamble. This means that table of contents and indexing information will become out of date as you continue to update the document file, but LaTeX will run faster. Unless you have a very slow LaTeX system, it is best not to issue a `\nofiles` command. The `.aux` file holds any references or citations you define (amongst other things) and is always generated by the `article`, `report` and `book` standard styles. You will find more information on cross referencing and bibliographic citation in Chapter 9.

5

Fonts and special symbols

LaTeX can produce normal type in eleven basic type styles and twelve sizes as well as a whole host of special symbols. It is particularly good at typesetting mathematics, because TeX understands the rules of mathematical typography and will automatically space formulae correctly. There are even special fonts which can be used for drawing diagrams and pictures.

This chapter is in two main parts which describe how to access fonts from within normal text mode and within maths mode. You will find commands for changing type size and style as well as tables of font sizes for the standard document styles, special accents for foreign languages, special punctuation symbols and mathematical symbols. A full discussion of maths typesetting is delayed until Chapter 8 and the picture drawing commands are described in Chapter 7.

You may find that there are TeX fonts on your system that are not part of the standard LaTeX font set. For instance, in my department the College shield is available for use on letterheads, business cards and so on. You will find instructions for accessing such fonts in section 5.4.

5.1 Normal text

In this context, 'normal text' means everything outside of maths mode, i.e. text that is not enclosed by $ ... $, \(... \), \[... \] or inside one of the maths-mode environments listed in Table 8.1.

5.1.1 Type styles

By default, LaTeX sets type in a font called 'roman'. There are seven type styles shown in Figure 5.1 that may be used with ordinary text — roman, **bold**, sans serif, *slanted*, *italic*, SMALL CAPS and `typewriter`. Style changing declarations are often embedded in braces so that at the end of a highlighted section the previous typestyle is automatically reselected, so for example

```
This {\bf bold} word
```

produces

This **bold** word

\rm	roman	abc ABC 012 +?-
\bf	**bold**	**abc ABC 012 +?-**
\sf	sans serif	abc ABC 012 +?-
\it	*italic*	*abc ABC 012 +?-*
\sl	*slanted*	*abc ABC 012 +?-*
\sc	SMALL CAPS	ABC ABC 012 +?-
\tt	typewriter	abc ABC 012 +?-

Table 5.1 Type styles

The typewriter style is especially useful because it is *non-proportionally spaced*. If you typeset a computer listing using \tt style then the spacing of the original will be preserved because all of the characters are the same width, just like on a typewriter or terminal. The other fonts are*proportionally spaced* so that an *i* takes up less space than an *m*.

5.1.2 Emphasised text

Most text is set in roman, with *occasional* sections emphasised in italics. This kind of emphasis can be used (sparingly please) to make a special point, or when a new technical term is being introduced for the first time. *Sometimes, emphasis is required* within *an emphasised passage which is conventionally represented by switching back into* roman. There is a special declaration \em which switches into italic if the current font is roman, and into roman if the current font is italic. Use this declaration for all emphasis. In general the \rm and \it declarations should rarely appear.

5.1.3 Ligatures

A ligature is two or more characters tied together into a single symbol. When text is properly typeset, combinations of characters such as ff should appear as the single symbol ff, so that riffraff becomes riffraff.

When TeX reads a source file it automatically looks for combinations of adjacent letters that would be better set as a single unit. The exact combinations are a property of the particular font in use and are supplied by the font designer. LaTeX is set up to look for the standard English ligatures listed in Table 5.2. Some other ligatures that are used in foreign languages are available (see Table 5.6) but must be explicitly asked for using the corresponding control sequence.

ff ff ff   fi fi fi   ffi ffi ffi   fl fl fl   ffl ffl ffl

Table 5.2 Automatically detected ligatures

In practice you can often spot documents that have been typeset by human printers because the ligatures are missing. This saves the typesetter time, and most customers do not know any better. Should you wish to simulate this barbarous practice, or to typeset an unusual word such as shelflife (which looks better as shelflife) then insert an empty group between the letters forming the ligature as in

> `half{}life` halflife.

5.1.4   Kerning

As well as actually replacing some letter combinations with ligatures, typesetters change the spacing between certain letter combinations so that, for instance in the word 'odd' the o and the d (which are both rather wide letters) are pushed apart, whereas in the word 'ox' the x is pulled in to the o. This process, known as *kerning*, keeps the visual density of words on the page even and makes your document more pleasant to read. As with ligaturing, all the kerning information is specified by the font designer and TEX automatically adjusts the spacing by looking for patterns in the text. No special commands are required.

5.1.5   Dashes

Printed books use four kinds of dashes and careful LATEX users will distinguish between them.

name	*typeset*	*command*	*usage*	*example*
hyphen	-	`-`	compound words	semi-precious
range dash	–	`--`	numeric range	pp 16–24
punctuation dash	—	`---`	asides	—or xyz—
minus sign	−	`$-$`	mathematics	$3 \times 6 - 2$

Table 5.3 Dashes

Some English readers find TEX's punctuation dash—which directly abuts neighbouring words—a little obtrusive, so I put a narrow space on either side — like this. You can make a narrow space with the command `\,` described in section 5.3.2.

5.1.6   Quote marks

A standard keyboard has three quote mark keys ‘ ’ and " . TEX produces ‘ ’ and ” for these characters. Most typists use only the " character so that quoted speech is printed ”like this” instead of "like this". In general you should forget all about the " key and just use ‘ and ’.

Single quotes are often used when a new technical term is being introduced. Double quotes are most often used for reported speech, with single quotes for reported speech within reported speech. LATEX uses the ligature mechanism to detect two quotes next to each other so that `` yields " not ". This causes a problem when nesting reported speech. ``He said `Do this''` produces "He said 'Do this"' because the first two close quotes are merged into a double quote. As before, the solution is use an empty group — ``He said `Do this'{}''` gives "He said 'Do this"'.

5.1.7 Logos

The TeX and LaTeX logos require unusual vertical spacing and may be produced with the `\LaTeX` and `\TeX` commands (note the unusual capitalisation).

5.1.8 Type sizes

The `\documentstyle` declaration at the start of your source file specifies a *font base size* for the typeset output. Character sizes are traditionally measured in *points*, of which there are approximately 72 in one inch. In LaTeX, the default size is usually 10pt, but the style may optionally provide other sizes. The standard document styles support 10pt, 11pt and 12pt base sizes.

The document styles define ten size changing declarations that may be used to scale your text from the base size. As long as you use these declarations then a change from an 11pt to a 12pt base size will cause all fonts to scale in step with each other. The size changing commands are named after the way in which LaTeX uses them. Table 5.4 shows the relative sizes obtained when using a 10pt base size.

`\tiny`	abc ABC 012 +?-
`\scriptsize`	abc ABC 012 +?-
`\footnotesize`	abc ABC 012 +?-
`\small`	abc ABC 012 +?-
`\normalsize`	abc ABC 012 +?-
`\large`	abc ABC 012 +?-
`\Large`	abc ABC 012 +?-
`\LARGE`	abc ABC 012 +?-
`\huge`	abc ABC 012 +?-
`\Huge`	abc ABC 012 +?-

Table 5.4 Size changing commands

Whenever you use a size changing command it resets the style to roman. Hence to get large bold characters you must use `\large\bf`. You can not use size changing commands in maths mode.

There is a new way of selecting fonts described in Chapter 13 that allows you to modify font attributes individually, and also gives access to many more fonts. It is not described in this chapter because this New Font Selection Scheme (NFSS) is not yet part of the standard distribution.

Naturally the exact font size corresponding to each of these depends on the base document font size. For the standard styles (`article`, `report` and `book`) the actual font sizes obtained are shown in Table 5.5.

Size command	[10pt]	[11pt]	[12pt]
\tiny	5pt	6pt	6pt
\scriptsize	7pt	8pt	8pt
\footnotesize	8pt	9pt	10pt
\small	9pt	10pt	11pt
\normalsize	10pt	11pt	12pt
\large	12pt	12pt	14pt
\Large	14pt	14pt	17pt
\LARGE	17pt	17pt	20pt
\huge	20pt	20pt	25pt
\Huge	25pt	25pt	25pt

Table 5.5 Font sizes using standard styles

5.1.9   Special symbols and foreign characters

Some common symbols are not represented in the normal computer character sets (such as the German ß). Others such as % are already reserved by LaTeX. Table 5.6 lists special symbols that can be accessed when typing normal text, and the control sequences that generate them. There are further table of maths-mode only symbols below.

#	\#	$	\$	%	\%	&	\&	–	_
{	\{	}	\}	¿	?`	¡	!`	£	\pounds
ø	\o	Ø	\O	ł	\l	Ł	\L	ß	\ss
†	\dag	‡	\ddag	§	\S	¶	\P	©	\copyright
å	\aa	ı	\i	j	\j	Å	\AA		
œ	\oe	Œ	\OE	æ	\ae	Æ	\AE		

Table 5.6 Special symbols and foreign characters

5.1.10   Foreign accents

Accents are produced by typesetting punctuation-like symbols, backspacing and typesetting the accented character. LaTeX provides a set of commands to do this such as \'e which generates the French e-acute é.

More generally, if the accent command is followed by a group then the accent is placed centrally over the group. The only accent that normally requires this facility is the tie which by definition must sit over more than one letter, so \t{oo} generates o͡o. The full set of accents is illustrated in Table 5.7. If you want to produce an accented *i* or *j* then the dot on the normal version of the character must be suppressed for which purpose the \i and \j commands, which produce ı and ȷ, are provided.

ò	\`o	ó	\'o	õ	\~o	ô	\^o	ǫ	\c o
ō	\=o	ȯ	\.o	o̲	\b o	o̦	\d o	o͡o	\t{oo}
ő	\H o	ŏ	\u o	ö	\"o	ǒ	\v o		

Table 5.7 Foreign accents

5.2   Maths mode text

Maths mode is described in some detail in Chapter 8. In maths mode TeX completely ignores the spacing in the source file and typesets according to its own rules. Many useful symbols are only available in maths mode. If you want these symbols in a paragraph set in normal mode, then switch temporarily into maths mode using single dollar signs to delimit the maths-mode text. In what follows, the mode changing commands are usually omitted.

5.2.1   Maths type styles

Most maths is set in a font called maths italic which is superficially like text italic, but more widely spaced. There are two type styles that are only available in maths mode — *maths italic*, and $\mathcal{CALLIGRAPHIC}$. In addition, maths may be printed in bold characters, and there are bold maths italic and bold calligraphic fonts for this purpose.

The calligraphic (or script) style provides capital letters only. If you attempt to typeset lowercase script, you will get bizarre results.

$\cal ABCDEFGHIJKLMNOPQRSTUVWXYZ$ produces

$\mathcal{ABCDEFGHIJKLMNOPQRSTUVWXYZ}$

Table 5.8 Calligraphic capitals

5.2.2   Bold maths

Bold maths can be switched on and off using the \boldmath and \unboldmath declarations. Perhaps unexpectedly, they must be used in text mode, not in maths mode. Normal maths italic characters, Greek, calligraphic and most special symbols will then be printed using bold characters. However, the following will always be set in normal (unbold) maths fonts

1. subscripts and superscripts

2. the variable sized symbols shown in Table 5.17

3. large delimiters from Table 5.18 (Normal sized versions *are* printed bold).

4. the characters + : ; ! ? ( ) [ ]

Some of the symbols in Table 5.16 are constructed by printing smaller symbols next to each other, such as \Longrightarrow $\Longrightarrow$ which is made up of = and ⇒. In bold maths mode, the spacing of the characters should be changed to ensure a neat join, but this does not always work.

5.2.3   Log-like functions

In maths mode, normal spacing is suppressed and each letter in a word is treated as a separate symbol, so no kerning or ligaturing is applied. If you need to typeset a function like $\sin(\theta)$ and you use the obvious $\sin(\theta)$ you will be disappointed to see $sin(\theta)$ appearing in the output. There are in fact a series of predefined functions listed in Table 5.9 that produce single words typeset in roman.

\arccos	\cos	\csc	\exp	\ker	\limsup	\min	\sinh
\arcsin	\cosh	\deg	\gcd	\lg	\ln	\Pr	\sup
\arctan	\cot	\det	\hom	\lim	\log	\sec	\tan
\arg	\coth	\dim	\inf	\liminf	\max	\sin	\tanh

Table 5.9 Log like functions

5.2.4   Maths accents

By analogy with the foreign accents listed in Table 5.7, LaTeX provides a separate set of accents for use in maths mode only shown in Table 5.10. Most of these reproduce foreign accents over a maths italic letter, but a vector accent is also provided. The difference between \hat and \widehat, and between \tilde and \widetilde is that the wide versions of the accent will attempt to stretch themselves over a long argument.

5.2.5   Greek characters

Upper and lower case Greek symbols may be accessed in maths mode. Table 5.11 shows the full set of letters. Note that several Greek capitals are the same as roman

˘x	\breve{x}	x́	\acute{x}	x̄	\bar{x}	ẋ	\dot{x}
x̌	\check{x}	x̀	\grave{x}	x⃗	\vec{x}	ẍ	\ddot{x}
x̂	\hat{x}	x̃	\tilde{x}	$\widehat{xyz}$	\widehat{xyz}	$\widetilde{xyz}$	\widetilde{xyz}

Table 5.10 Maths accents

capitals, and that some lowercase Greek letters have alternative forms. Uppercase Greek is traditionally set using unslanted characters. Italic Greek capitals are available *via* the \mit declaration.

α	\alpha			A	A	A	A
β	\beta			B	B	B	B
γ	\gamma			Γ	\Gamma	Γ	\mit\Gamma
δ	\delta			Δ	\Delta	Δ	\mit\Delta
ε	\epsilon	ε	\varepsilon	E	E	E	E
ζ	\zeta			Z	Z	Z	Z
η	\eta			H	H	H	H
θ	\theta	ϑ	\vartheta	Θ	\Theta	Θ	\mit\Theta
ι	\iota			I	I	I	I
κ	\kappa			K	K	K	K
λ	\lambda			Λ	\Lambda	Λ	\mit\Lambda
μ	\mu			M	M	M	M
ν	\nu			N	N	N	N
ξ	\xi			Ξ	\Xi	Ξ	\mit\Xi
o	o			O	O	O	O
π	\pi	ϖ	\varpi	Π	\Pi	Π	\mit\Pi
ρ	\rho	ϱ	\varrho	P	P	P	P
σ	\sigma	ς	\varsigma	Σ	\Sigma	Σ	\mit\Sigma
τ	\tau			T	T	T	T
υ	\upsilon			Υ	\Upsilon	Υ	\mit\Upsilon
φ	\phi	φ	\varphi	Φ	\Phi	Φ	\mit\Phi
χ	\chi			X	X	X	X
ψ	\psi			Ψ	\Psi	Ψ	\mit\Psi
ω	\omega			Ω	\Omega	Ω	\mit\Omega

Table 5.11 Greek letters

5.2.6   Other mathematical symbols

A large set of operators, relations and delimiters are shown in Tables 5.12–5.18. Each class of operators has a *type* which governs the spacing rules applied by LaTeX when typesetting formulae. The rules governing this spacing are described in Chapter 8, but for now note that the *symbol* \vert (|) is not the same as the *relation* \mid or the delimiter |. All three commands produce the same character, but surrounded by different amounts of space.

The delimiters and variable size operators listed in Tables 5.17 and 5.18 are available in different sizes. Chapter 8 shows you how to get variable size symbols.

ℵ	\aleph	ℜ	\Re	ℑ	\Im	℧	\mho
ℏ	\hbar	℘	\wp	ı	\imath	ȷ	\jmath
ℓ	\ell	∇	\nabla	∂	\partial	√	\surd
∀	\forall	∃	\exists	¬	\neg or \lnot	\	\backslash
⊤	\top	⊥	\bot	‖	| or \Vert	∠	\angle
♣	\clubsuit	◇	\diamondsuit	♡	\heartsuit	♠	\spadesuit
′	\prime	∅	\emptyset	∞	\infty	|	\vert
♭	\flat	♮	\natural	♯	\sharp		
□	\Box	◇	\Diamond	△	\triangle		

Table 5.12 Miscellaneous symbols of type ORD

+	+	−	-	/	/	÷	\div
∗	\ast	⋆	\star	·	\cdot	×	\times
∘	\circ	◯	\bigcirc	•	\bullet	⊙	\odot
⊕	\oplus	⊖	\ominus	⊗	\otimes	⊘	\oslash
∩	\cap	∪	\cup	⊓	\sqcap	⊔	\sqcup
⊎	\uplus	◁	\triangleleft	▷	\triangleright	±	\pm
◇	\diamond	△	\bigtriangleup	▽	\bigtriangledown	∓	\mp
◁	\lhd	▷	\rhd	⊴	\unlhd	⊵	\unrhd
∨	\vee or \lor	∧	\wedge or \land	\	\setminus	≀	\wr
†	\dagger	‡	\ddagger	∐	\amalg		

Table 5.13 Binary operations of type BIN

5.3 Leaving space in a document

You can leave horizontal and vertical space with the commands \hspace{*length*} and \vspace{*length*}. *length* can be any construction described in Section 11.3.

If an \hspace occurs at a line break, or a \vspace command occurs at a page break, it is suppressed so as to avoid anomalous gaps at the start of lines and pages. The *-forms of these commands \hspace* and \vspace* will always generate space even if they fall at a break.

The command \par produces exactly the same effect as a blank line: it marks the end of a paragraph. Immediately after a \par command or a blank line, you can use

$<$	$<$	$>$	$>$	$=$	$=$
$\leq$	\leq or \le	$\geq$	\geq or \ge	$\equiv$	\equiv
$\prec$	\prec	$\succ$	\succ	$\sim$	\sim
$\preceq$	\preceq	$\succeq$	\succeq	$\simeq$	\simeq
$\ll$	\ll	$\gg$	\gg	$\asymp$	\asymp
$\subset$	\subset	$\supset$	\supset	$\approx$	\approx
$\subseteq$	\subseteq	$\supseteq$	\supseteq	$\cong$	\cong
$\sqsubseteq$	\sqsubseteq	$\sqsupseteq$	\sqsupseteq	$\bowtie$	\bowtie
$\in$	\in	$\ni$	\ni or \owns	$\propto$	\propto
$\vdash$	\vdash	$\dashv$	\dashv	$\models$	\models
$\smile$	\smile	$\mid$	\mid	$\doteq$	\doteq
$\frown$	\frown	$\parallel$	\parallel	$\perp$	\perp

Table 5.14 Relations of type REL

$\not<$	\not<	$\not>$	\not>	$\neq$	\not= or \ne or \neq
$\not\leq$	\not\leq	$\not\geq$	\not\geq	$\not\equiv$	\not\equiv
$\not\prec$	\not\prec	$\not\succ$	\not\succ	$\not\sim$	\not\sim
$\not\preceq$	\not\preceq	$\not\succeq$	\not\succeq	$\not\simeq$	\not\simeq
$\not\ll$	\not\ll	$\not\gg$	\not\gg	$\not\asymp$	\not\asymp
$\not\subset$	\not\subset	$\not\supset$	\not\supset	$\not\approx$	\not\approx
$\not\subseteq$	\not\subseteq	$\not\supseteq$	\not\supseteq	$\not\cong$	\not\cong
$\not\sqsubseteq$	\not\sqsubseteq	$\not\sqsupseteq$	\not\sqsupseteq	$\not\bowtie$	\not\bowtie

Table 5.15 Negated relations of type REL

$\leftarrow$	\leftarrow or \gets	$\longleftarrow$	\longleftarrow	$\uparrow$	\uparrow
$\Leftarrow$	\Leftarrow	$\Longleftarrow$	\Longleftarrow	$\Uparrow$	\Uparrow
$\rightarrow$	\rightarrow or \to	$\longrightarrow$	\longrightarrow	$\downarrow$	\downarrow
$\Rightarrow$	\Rightarrow	$\Longrightarrow$	\Longrightarrow	$\Downarrow$	\Downarrow
$\leftrightarrow$	\leftrightarrow	$\longleftrightarrow$	\longleftrightarrow	$\updownarrow$	\updownarrow
$\Leftrightarrow$	\Leftrightarrow	$\Longleftrightarrow$	\Longleftrightarrow	$\Updownarrow$	\Updownarrow
$\mapsto$	\mapsto	$\longmapsto$	\longmapsto	$\nearrow$	\nearrow
$\hookleftarrow$	\hookleftarrow	$\hookrightarrow$	\hookrightarrow	$\searrow$	\searrow
$\leftharpoonup$	\leftharpoonup	$\rightharpoonup$	\rightharpoonup	$\swarrow$	\swarrow
$\leftharpoondown$	\leftharpoondown	$\rightharpoondown$	\rightharpoondown	$\nwarrow$	\nwarrow
$\rightleftharpoons$	\rightleftharpoons	$\leadsto$	\leadsto		

Table 5.16 Arrows of type REL

∑	\sum	∩	\bigcap	⊙	\bigodot
∏	\prod	∪	\bigcup	⊗	\bigotimes
∐	\coprod	⊔	\bigsqcup	⊕	\bigoplus
∫	\int	⋁	\bigvee	⨄	\biguplus
∮	\oint	⋀	\bigwedge		

Table 5.17 Variable size operators of type OP

(	(	)	)	↑	\uparrow
[	[	]	]	↓	\downarrow
{	\{	}	\}	↕	\updownarrow
⌊	\lfloor	⌋	\rfloor	⇑	\Uparrow
⌈	\lceil	⌉	\rceil	⇓	\Downarrow
⟨	\langle	⟩	\rangle	⇕	\Updownarrow
/	/	\	\backslash		
|	|	‖	\\|		

Table 5.18 Delimiters of types OPEN and CLOSE

the special command \addvspace{*length*} which will 'top-up' the vertical space to *length*. This command will only add space if necessary and many environments add vertical space of their own, so the effect of an \addvspace command is to ensure that *at least length* worth of vertical space will be left.

5.3.1 Standard vertical spaces

Each style file defines three vertical intervals that are used throughout the document when setting displays out from their enclosing text, spacing paragraphs and so on. The commands \bigskip, \medskip and \smallskip generate these standard spaces, and should be used in preference to explicit lengths so as preserve the overall look and feel of the document.

5.3.2 Standard horizontal spaces

A backslash followed by a space (in other words the control symbol '\ ') produces an interword space that may be broken just like an ordinary space. It is needed when a space must be left after a control word because TeX eats all normal space after a control word. Hence the many occurrences of the LaTeX logo in this document are typed as \LaTeX\ .

The following horizontal space making commands are available in maths mode

\, thin space ‖

\: medium space ‖

\; thick space ‖

\! thin backspace

\quad a quad (1em) | |

\qquad a double quad (2em) | |

The thin space command \, and quad commands may also be used in text mode. A common use is to space the quotation marks in nested reported speech ''He said, 'Do this'\,'' produces "He said, 'Do this'".

5.3.3 Springs and leaders

There is a special command that can be used in the *length* parameter of the spacing commands. A length of \fill means 'as much as you need' and is like inserting a *spring* into a line. Items neighbouring a spring are pushed up against the margins, so

        left flushed text \hspace{\fill} right flushed text

produces

    left flushed text   right flushed text

Similarly, vertical \fills may be used to spread paragraphs vertically. If you put two or more springs on a line you can get special spacing effects. These are demonstrated in section 11.4.2.

The command \hfill is an abbreviation for \hspace{\fill}, and the commands \dotfill and \hrulefill also produce springs, except that their position is marked by a line of dots and an underline rule respectively:

        left flushed text \dotfill right flushed text
        left flushed text \hrulefill right flushed text

produces

    left flushed text .... right flushed text
    left flushed text _____right flushed text

5.3.4 Space after full stops

Normally LaTeX leaves a small space after a full stop. It would be undesirable to have space after every full stop, since abbreviations such as U.S.A. would then be spread out. Therefore the rule applied is: leave a space only if a full stop follows a word beginning with a lowercase letter.

Most of the time this works well. There are occasions however when a sentence ends with a capitalised word, and in such cases you must follow the full stop with the command \@ which explicitly generates the end of sentence space, as in She saw John Smith.\@

The \frenchspacing command completely suppresses all extra space after punctuation. Default behaviour is restored with the \nonfrenchspacing declaration.

Name		LATEX	Sample
CMR10	Roman	\rm	abc ABC 123 ?!()
CMSL10	Slanted	\sl	*abc ABC 123 ?!()*
CMTI10	Text Italic	\it	*abc ABC 123 ?!()*
CMU10	Upright		*abc ABC 123 ?!()*
CMB10	Bold		**abc ABC 123 ?!()**
CMBX10	Bold Extended	\bf	**abc ABC 123 ?!()**
CMBXSL10	Bold Extended Slanted		***abc ABC 123 ?!()***
CMBXTI10	Bold Extended Text Italic		***abc ABC 123 ?!()***
CMCSC10	Caps and Small Caps	\sc	ABC ABC 123 ?!()
CMDUNH10	Dunhill		abc ABC 123 ?!()
CMSS10	Sans Serif	\sf	abc ABC 123 ?!()
CMSSI10	Sans Serif Italic		*abc ABC 123 ?!()*
CMSSBX10	Sans Serif Bold Extended		**abc ABC 123 ?!()**
CMTT10	Teletype	\tt	abc ABC 123 ?!()
CMSLTT10	Slanted Teletype		abc ABC 123 ?!()
CMITT10	Italic Teletype		abc ABC 123 ?!()
CMTCSC10	Teletype Caps and Small Caps		ABC ABC 123 ?!()

Table 5.19 Common Computer Modern fonts

5.3.5 Space after italics

Switching between italic and upright fonts can lead to ugly text if the last italic character has an ascender, which may collide with the next word or punctuation mark: '*PS*:' should really be typeset as '*PS*:'. Every TEX italic font has a special space value associated with it called the *italic correction* which you can typeset using the command \/.

5.4 Accessing other TEX fonts

Although LATEX provides a large set of characters and symbols most TEX installations will have even more available in different fonts and sizes.

If you want to use these you must first tell LATEX about them with the command \newfont{*command*}{*fontdescription*}. For instance, the section titles in this book are set in a 12pt bold sans serif font which is not part of LATEX's standard repertoire. It is declared using \newfont{\sfb}{cmssbx10} after which

\sfb abc ABC 012 +?- produces **abc ABC 012 +?-**

You should be restrained in your use of 'alien' fonts, since there is no guarantee that other LATEX users will have access to them. If you write documents for distribution to other people, stick to the standard commands. However, most TEX installations include the set of fonts shown in Figure 5.19 in various sizes.

cmr17:
abcdefg ABCDEFG 0123456 !?()

cmr10 magnified to 17pt:
abcdefg ABCDEFG 0123456 !?()

Figure 5.1 17pt characters

5.4.1   Font magnifications

Every TeX font has a *design size* which is its natural size on the page. Larger characters are best obtained by using variants of the font with larger design sizes, because the details of serifs and curves will in general vary slightly with the size to produce a balanced composition.

Figure 5.1 shows sample characters from the CMR17 font which has a design size of 17pt, and from the CMR10 font magnified to 17pt size. As you can see, the CMR10 characters are slightly wider and heavier than the true 17pt characters. This variation maintains print density and readability between different size fonts. Always use the font with a design size nearest the size you need on the typeset output.

If you must magnify a font because you do not have the necessary design sizes, there are two ways to go about it: either by requesting a specific size (usually in points) or by *scaling* the font by a magnification factor. Scaling is preferred, because there are seven standard scaling factors which are predefined for you to match the available font magnifications. If you specify an absolute size, you may miscalculate and request a non-standard height which is not available.

Fonts are usually scaled by a factor of 1.2, with a base size of 10pt. A standard set of sizes is then:

5.787 6.944 8.333 $\boxed{10}$ 12 14.4 17.28 20.736 24.883 29.86 35.831 42.998 51.598

These are loosely referred to as 5pt, 7pt, 9pt and so on by rounding to the nearest integer. In TeX parlance, each factor 1.2 magnification is a *magstep*, and there are seven predefined commands \magstep0 – \magstep5 and \magstephalf which apply scalings of 0, 1.2, 14.4 ... 24.883, and in the case of \magstephalf 1.1. You use the commands when specifying the fonts. In Figure 5.1 the magnified CMR10 font was declared as

```
\newfont{\bigcmr}{CMR10 scaled \magstep3}
```

to magnify 10pt characters up to 17.28pt. The word scaled here is a keyword (see section 2.1.5) and has no leading \.

You can also request font magnification by absolute size: the same effect could be achieved with

```
\newfont{\bigcmr}{CMR10 at 17.28pt}
```

The only problem with using absolute sizes is that it is easy to forget the decimal places, and request a font that that has a non-standard size. TEX will proceed quite happily, but when you come to run the DVI driver you may find that the font is unavailable.

5.4.2 Accessing characters by number

Some fonts, such as the maths fonts, contain symbols rather than letters, and unless someone has defined control sequences that access the individual characters you may not be able to typeset them. If you can get a list of the characters and their positions within the font you can use the \symbol command to access them. For instance, the æ diphthong character is in fact character number 26 in the standard alphabetic fonts, so you can typeset one either with the usual command \ae or with \symbol{26}.

5.4.3 How to find out what fonts are available

Font information is stored in two sets of files: *TEX font metric files* which have a file type of .tfm, and *pixel files* which have file types of either .pk, .pxl or .gf. The pk format files are now standard and if your system is using either of the other two formats you should consider switching over, because pk files are more space and processing time efficient.

TEX itself only needs the .tfm files to run. These files list the size of bounding box for every character in the font. Since TEX is really a program for putting boxes together and does not need to know the pattern of ink to be found within each box, the .tfm file is sufficient.

The DVI driver that produces the printer file clearly *does* need to know the pattern of ink, and that information is held in the pixel files. The reason that separate sets of files are maintained is that a single small .tfm file holds all the information that TEX needs, whereas the pixel files can become very large, especially when high resolution devices are used. This book was drafted using a normal laser printer with manageably small pixel files, but the final copy was produced on a high resolution phototypesetter that needs ten times as much file space to hold the pixel files. To make matters worse, every magnification of a font requires a separate pixel file, so it is not uncommon for the more obscure fonts to only be available in the smaller magnifications.

The list of .tfm files tells you what fonts TEX will recognise, and the list of pixel files tells you what magnifications are available for printing. On most systems, there is a fonts directory parallel to the inputs directory (see page 24) which contains the .tfm and pixel files. If you find that a font is not available at the desired magnification it may be possible to make the necessary pixel files using the METAFONT program. You will find more information on how to obtain unusual fonts in Chapter 13.

6

Text displays

A piece of text that is typeset so as to stand out as a separate block from the main text is called a *display*. They are used for lists, large quotations and for temporarily overriding text justification. LaTeX provides a series of environments for generating different kinds of displays.

The `center`, `flushleft` and `flushright` environments change the justification, so that instead of spreading the lines of text out to meet the two margins the text lines are centred, given a ragged right or a ragged left. Some people prefer a ragged right for letters, which looks a little less formal. The address box in the example letter shown in Figure 3.1 has been set using a `flushright` environment to give a ragged left.

There are three environments for indenting displays. They all leave a little vertical space above and below the display body. Within a `quote` environment, the margins are indented and the paragraph indentation is suppressed. The `quotation` environment is very similar but uses normal paragraph indentation. It is intended for longer, multiparagraph quotes. The `verse` environment is intended for type setting verse. It indents, and sets a ragged right.

Lists may be constructed with three different environments. `itemize` constructs bulleted lists, `enumerate` makes numbered lists and `description` uses text labels. Within any of these three, the `\item` command is used to define the start of a new list body.

Finally, text may be set 'as-is' without any interpretation of commands using the `verbatim` and `verbatim*` environments. Even spacing is maintained within a `verbatim` environment, which makes them especially useful for including computer programs, where the indentation is often significant and must be maintained in the typeset text. There is also an inline verbatim command called `\verb` which may be used in the body of the text without introducing any vertical spacing.

6.1 Indented displays

Indentation is useful for far more than just quotations. The creative use of white space in your document can make it pleasant to read, and indented paragraphs reinforcing important points stand out well.

6.1.1   quote

A short quotation may be represented in the main text simply by putting quote marks around it — "Be concise in your writing and talking, especially when giving instructions to others.". However, for long quotations this can often result in complicated and difficult to read paragraphs. A display uses white space to break up the text and make it easier to read. The quote environment indents paragraphs and leaves a vertical gap

> 'The less a thing can be proved, the angrier we get when we argue about it.'

> 'Money cannot buy happiness, but it can make you awfully comfortable while you're being miserable.'

6.1.2   quotation

If a quote contains several paragraphs then use the quotation environment which preserves paragraph indentation and spacing.

> I thought the following four would be enough, provided that I made a firm and constant resolution not to fail in the observance of them.
>
> The first was never to accept anything as true if I had not evident knowledge of its being so; that is carefully avoid precipitancy and prejudice, and to embrace in my judgement only what presented itself to my mind so clearly and distinctly that I had no occasion to doubt it. The second, to divide each problem I examined into as many parts as was feasible, and as was requisite for its better solution. The third, to direct my thoughts in an orderly way; beginning with the simplest objects, those most apt to be known, and ascending little by little, in steps as it were, to the knowledge of the complex; and establishing an order in thought even when the objects had no natural priority one to another. And the last, to make throughout such complete enumerations and such general surveys that I might be sure of leaving nothing out.
>
> René Descartes, *Discours de la méthode pour bien conduire sa raison et chercher la vérité dans les sciences* 1637

6.1.3   verse

The verse environment indents the margins and suppresses line justification leaving a ragged right. You must mark the end of each line with a \\ command.

> A king who was mad at the time,
> Decreed limerick writing a crime;
> But late in the night
> All the poets would write
> Verses without any rhyme or meter.

6.2   Non-justified displays

When TeX builds a paragraph it collects words together until it has enough to almost fill a line, and then *justifies* the line. It does this by adjusting the interword spacing, experimenting with hyphenating the last word, and adding one more word until it finds the least bad layout.

Sometimes a *non-justified* paragraph is required in which case TeX simply gathers words until the addition of one more would extend the line beyond the right margin and then goes straight on to the next line. In general this will generate a 'ragged right' paragraph.

There are three LaTeX environments that produce unjustified text

◇ `flushleft` which flushes text against the left margin thus giving a ragged right,

◇ `flushright` which gives a ragged left (rarely required),

◇ `center` which centres the line by distributing the left over space equally between the right and left ends.

Their effects are illustrated in Table 6.1.

flushleft	center	flushright
Mary had a little lamb	Mary had a little lamb	Mary had a little lamb
She tied it to a pylon	She tied it to a pylon	She tied it to a pylon
10kV was all it took	10kV was all it took	10kV was all it took
To turn its wool to nylon	To turn its wool to nylon	To turn its wool to nylon

Table 6.1 Non-justified displays

6.3   List making displays

6.3.1   enumerate

A list of recommendations might be labelled in numerical order. The `enumerate` environment illustrated in Figure 6.1 typesets numbered blocks marked with `\item` commands. By default, the outermost display is numbered using arabic numerals and nested displays using parenthesised lower case letters, lower case roman numerals and capitalised letters in that order.

You should be restrained in your use of nested lists as they quickly become hard to follow. LaTeX provides four levels of nested `enumerate` environments, which is probably more than you should ever use.

1. First item of outermost list

   (a) Start level 2

      i. Start level 3

         A. Start level 4

          – Optional label

         B. End level 4

   (b) End of level 2

2. End of list

```
\begin{enumerate}
\item First item of outermost list
\begin{enumerate}
\item Start level 2
\begin{enumerate}
\item Start level 3
\begin{enumerate}
\item Start level 4
\item[--] Optional label
\item End level 4
\end{enumerate}
\end{enumerate}
\item End of level 2
\end{enumerate}
\item End of list
\end{enumerate}
```

Figure 6.1 Nested enumerate environments

You can use an optional argument on the \item command in an enumerate environment to override the numeric label. Incrementing of the label counter is suppressed in this case.

6.3.2 itemize

If you want to summarise a series of points you might

- write a series of punchy sentences

- put them in a list

- put a bullet before each item

This is exactly what an itemize environment does for you. The lines are introduced with an \item command. An optional argument to the \item command lets you specify another character to be used instead of the bullet. Popular alternatives include

◊ \item[$\diamond$]

◊ \item[$\diamondsuit$]

▷ \item[$\triangleright$]

∗ \item[$\ast$]

⋆ \item[$\star$]

○ \item[$\circ$]

- First item of outermost list
  - Start level 2
    * Start level 3
      · Start level 4
        – Optional label
      · End level 4
  - End of level 2
- End of list

```
\begin{itemize}
\item First item of outermost list
\begin{itemize}
\item Start level 2
\begin{itemize}
\item Start level 3
\begin{itemize}
\item Start level 4
\item[--] Optional label
\item End level 4
\end{itemize}
\end{itemize}
\item End of level 2
\end{itemize}
\item End of list
\end{itemize}
```

Figure 6.2 Nested itemize environments

□ `\item[$\Box$]`

The standard markers are shown in Figure 6.2, which is equivalent to Figure 6.1 except that the `enumerate` environments have been replaced with `itemize`.

6.3.3   description

If you use the `description` environment you can specify a word as an item label, which will then be typeset in `\bf` with a small following space:

itemize has a column of labels and inset paragraphs of text,

description starts labels at the left margin and the text picks up immediately after the label.

6.4   Verbatim displays

LaTeX's interpretation of source text sometimes gets in the way. In particular, if you want to accurately represent a computer program (like the examples in this book) it would be convenient to completely disable all commands. The `verbatim` environment typesets using the fixed spacing `\tt` font and preserves all line breaks and space characters in the source. All commands are ignored until an `\end{verbatim}` is encountered.

The `verbatim*` environment is identical to `verbatim` except that spaces are typeset using the ␣ character. In fact, spaces are stripped from the *ends* of lines, so the typeset text will not be an exact representation of the source text.

Often, it is useful to have some verbatim text in-line with normal text. Many of the examples in this book are presented in this way. The command

The `verbatim` environment:

```
line1
line2 with trailing spaces
```

The `verbatim*` environment

```
line1
line2␣with␣trailing␣spaces
```

Inline verbatim text:
`inline verb test`   and
`inline␣verb*␣test␣␣`

```
The {\tt verbatim} environment:
\begin{verbatim}
line1
line2 with trailing spaces

\end{verbatim}


The {\tt verbatim*} environment
\begin{verbatim*}
line1
line2 with trailing spaces
\end{verbatim*}


Inline verbatim text:\\
\verb|inline verb test   | and\\
\verb*|inline verb* test  |
```

Figure 6.3 Verbatim commands and environments

```
\verbdelimiter-character text delimiter-character
```

looks at the character immediately following (the *delimiter-character*) and then
switches into verbatim mode until the next occurrence of that character. Naturally,
this means that the verbatim *text* may not contain the *delimiter-character*.
You may not use the * character as a delimiter. A popular convention is to use
| characters to delimit *text* because they stand out well in the source file. There
is also a `\verb*` command that works the same way as `\verb`, but which replaces
spaces with ␣ characters. The four verbatim commands are illustrated in Figure 6.3.

The `verbatim` environments can only cope with a few pages of text before they
overflow, which can be a problem if you want to include a long program listing. You
can split it up into several concatenated environments, but LaTeX inserts a blank
line between two adjacent `verbatim` environments, upsetting the vertical spacing.
In Chapter 13 some replacement `verbatim` style files are described which solve
this problem, and allow a file to be included in verbatim mode, optionally with
automatic line number generation.

6.5   Problems with display spacing

Displays sometimes generate unexpected spacing. These are the rules:

1. All displays start on a new line (not a new paragraph unless, of course the
   line before the display is blank or a `\par` has been issued).

2. The text following a display starts on a new line (not a new paragraph unless,
   of course, the line after the display is blank or a `\par` has been issued).

3. If a right brace or some other \end command follows a display, then the following text will be given a paragraph indentation, even though it is not the start of a new paragraph. This can be suppressed with a \noindent command at the start of the text.

4. If a text display finishes with a maths display (see Chapter 8) then extra vertical space may be inserted. This situation should be avoided, but if necessary a command of the form \vspace{-0.5cm} may be used to vertically backspace.

6.6   Making new kinds of lists

All of the environments described in this chapter are defined in terms of the underlying list environment and its parameters which is described in Chapter 11. You can define your own list making environments based around list using the \newenvironment command described in Chapter 10.

7

Tables, figures and pictures

Typesetting tables is often the most taxing part of formatting a document, and human typists and printers charge extra for such material. LaTeX provides two environments for tabular material — tabbing which simulates the behaviour of a simple typewriter with tabulation stops and tabular which can produce complex tables with frames and intercolumn lines.

Illustrations and tables are conventionally placed at the top of a page or on a page of their own. These insertions are called 'floats' because a figure or table can float away from the point at which it is referenced. LaTeX has two float environments figure and table and will automatically generate captions and numbers for these as well as collating lists of tables and figures for insertion immediately after the contents.

LaTeX also has an environment for drawing pictures. The capabilities are rather limited because the pictures are drawn using a predefined set of special symbol characters, limiting you to certain line angles and thicknesses. As long as the picture environment is good enough for your diagram, you benefit from having the graphics integrated with the text and from the use of exactly the same fonts in your diagram and in the text.

7.1 The tabbing environment

Within a tabbing environment you can set tab stops and then tabulate to them, as well as indenting the left margin. The text of a tabbing environment comprises a sequence of rows terminated by \\ or \kill commands. Within a row, columns are separated by the tabulation commands that are described below. Each of these column entries constitutes a separate scope region, so any declarations issued within a tabbing environment will be lost at the next tabbing command or line end. You must not nest tabbing environments. Figure 7.1 illustrates most of the features of the tabbing environment which are described below.

7.1.1 Setting tabs

The \= command sets a tab stop. Tab stops are numbered in the order in which they are set, which is not necessarily the sequence in which they appear across the page since you can backspace using a negative \hspace command between tab setting commands.

10 off	bits	£0.70
13 off	bytes	£5.60
		£6.30
17.5% VAT		£1.10
		£7.40

```
\begin{tabbing}
Please supply:
000 off\= items \=\pounds10.00\kill
10 off\>bits\>\pounds0.70\\
13 off\>bytes\>\pounds5.60 \+\+\\
\pounds6.30\\[2ex]
17.5\% VAT \'\pounds1.10\\
\pounds7.40\\
\end{tabbing}
```

Figure 7.1 The `tabbing` environment

Often it is convenient to use a sample line to set the tab stops at the beginning of a tabular environment without actually producing any output. If you finish a line with a `\kill` instead of a `\\` command then the output of that line is discarded keeping the effects of any tab `\=` commands.

7.1.2 Moving between tabs

The `\>` moves the current position to the next tab stop. Unlike a typewriter, reverse motion may sometimes result since as noted above, tab stops may be set in a non-left to right order. In addition, if the text in a column overruns the next tab position, a `\>` command will still move the current position to that tab stop even though the text in the two columns will then be superimposed.

7.1.3 Indenting and outdenting

Normally a `\\` or `\kill` command starts a new line, resetting the horizontal position to the left text margin. *Indenting* means temporarily moving the left margin in one tab position. Outdenting is the reverse process.

`\+` indents the left margin one tab stop. It is equivalent to inserting one `\>` command at the start of each subsequent row. Multiple `\+` commands have a cumulative effect.

`\-` outdents the left margin by one tab stop, cancelling the effect of one preceding `\+` command.

`\<` may be used at the beginning of a row *only* to generate a temporary outdent of one stop for that line only.

7.1.4 Saving tab stop settings

The present tab setting may be saved using a `\pushtabs` command which also clears all tab stops. The old settings are restored by a `\poptabs` command. These command may be nested but must appear in matching pairs within a single `tabbing` environment. They cannot be used to save tab settings between `tabbing` environments.

Country	Closing	↕
	market rates	
Australia	2.4880–2.4920	0.2
Austria	20.70–20.73	-0.4
Belgium	60.47–60.70	-1.0
		-1.2

```
\begin{tabular}
{l|r@{--}lr}
Country&
\multicolumn{2}{c}{Closing}&
\multicolumn{1}{c}{$\updownarrow$}\\
&\multicolumn{2}{c}{market rates}&\\
\hline
Australia&2.4880&2.4920&0.2\\
Austria&20.70&20.73&-0.4\\
Belgium&60.47&60.70&-1.0\\
\cline{4-4}
\multicolumn{3}{c}{~}&-1.2\\
\cline{4-4}
\end{tabular}
```

Figure 7.2 The tabular environment

7.1.5 Special alignment commands

The \` command must be the last tabbing command in a row before the \\ terminator. The remaining text of the row is set flushright against the right margin.

The \' command allows text to hang back into the last column. All of the text between a preceding tabbing command and the \' command is set flush right against the preceding tab stop. A gap of width \tabbingsep is left between the end of the flushright text and the actual tab stop. This operation is best understood with reference to the example in Figure 7.1.

7.1.6 Accents in tabbing mode

The \', \` and \= commands are usually used to produce accents. Within a tabbing environment they are renamed \a', \a` and \a= respectively. The \- command also has another meaning — it is used to indicate a discretionary hyphen within a paragraph (i.e. a point where a line break may be taken), but this has no meaning within a tabbing environment because all lines must be explicitly terminated so no alternative is needed.

7.2 The tabular environment

Tab stops are useful, but they are no substitute for a properly set table — compare the quality of tables produced on a typewriter to those in books. Typically *rules* are used to mark off parts of a table, and entries may be centred or flushed right (especially in financial tables) as well as possibly spanning several columns.

The tabular environment provides many powerful facilities in an easy to use format. An example that demonstrates most of the features is shown in Figure 7.2.

Each `tabular` environment produces a single box which must fit on a page. If you need to maintain column widths across several pages, then try the `tabbing` environment, or manually split your table into several `tabular` environments.

7.2.1　`tabular` **environment parameters**

There are two `tabular` environments:

> \begin{tabular}[*alignment*]{*columns*} *rows* \end{tabular}
>
> \begin{tabular*}{*width*}[*alignment*]{*columns*} *rows* \end{tabular*}

The two environments behave identically except that the *-form has a preset *width* and the normal form adjusts itself to the width of the longest line of the table. There must be stretchable space within the rows of `tabular*` environment to allow the columns to expand.

The optional *alignment* parameters specify the vertical positioning of the resulting box. The default is that the center of the box is aligned with the current text line, [t] aligns with the top of the box so that the table hangs down below line and [b] aligns with the bottom. If the table is set in a paragraph of its own (as is usual) the parameter has no meaning.

7.2.2　**Column formatting commands**

The *columns* parameter comprises a number of column formatting commands each of which specifies a single column in the table and its justification mode. Optionally, fixed text may be inserted automatically between columns. The following may appear within a *columns* argument

l a left aligned column

c a centred column

r a right justified column

| a vertical line running the full height of the table

p{*width*} a column of paragraphs set in a box of the given *width*.

@{*text*} arbitrary LATEX text that is used to replace the usual intercolumn space. Command appearing within an @-expression may need a preceding \protect command.

7.2.3　**Row formatting commands**

Within the environment, the *rows* are separated by \\ commands and comprise a sequence of column entries separated by & characters. The column entries form separate scope regions, so declarations made within a column entry will be lost at the next & or \\.

Blank fields are perfectly allowable, so a blank row in the table may be generated with a run of blank fields: a `tabular` environment with three columns would require a line of the form &&\\. If there are fewer & column separators in the row than required by the column formatting parameter then LaTeX will continue without raising an error, but any trailing | commands in the column formatting parameter will be lost. Too many & characters *is* an error, and the first excess & will be converted to a \\ command and an error message issued.

7.2.4   Spanning multiple columns

Sometimes it is useful to be able to set a row item that spans several columns of the main table. In Figure 7.2 the Closing and market rates fields span the two numeric fields below them. This is achieved using a command of the form

> \multicolumn{*numbcols*}{*format*}{*text*}

The *text* will be typeset in a box spanning the next *numbcols* columns. The *format* command uses the column formatting commands described in section 7.2.2 to specify the layout of the multicolumn field. Any | commands in the main tabular environment column formatting parameter will be suppressed in a \multicolumn field, so the *format* parameter must reinstate them if necessary.

7.2.5   Placing horizontal rules

A full width line may be placed across the whole table with an \hline command. The command must appear *between* or before or after rows of the table — it may not appear before a \\ command for instance.

The sub-total lines in Figure 7.2 only span a single column. The command

> \cline{*startcolumn* - *endcolumn*}

draws a horizontal rule spanning *startcolumn* to *endcolumn* inclusive. The - in the parameter must appear. As with the \hline command, \cline may only appear outside of any row specifications, as shown in Figure 7.2.

7.2.6   Adding extra vertical rules

Within a row specification, and within @-expressions, a \vline command can be used to create a vertical rule the height of the row. The rule does not extend across the entire table, but corresponding \vrule commands on successive rows will match up. Normally, LaTeX automatically adds intercolumn space, so that the rule generated by \vrule will not align itself with rules created using | commands in the column formatting parameter to the tabular environment. However, an \hspace{\fill} spring command may be used to force the rule over to either end of the row item.

7.3   Floats

LaTeX provides two environments for floating bodies — table and figure. They are essentially identical except that table uses captions of the form **Table 1.3** and make entries on the list of tables (.lot) file whilst figure uses **Figure** ... and makes entries on the list of figures (.lof) file. Each environment has a *-form that makes floats span both columns in a [twocolumn] document.

\begin{figure}[*location*] *text* \end{figure}

\begin{figure*}[*location*] *text* \end{figure*}

\begin{table}[*location*] *text* \end{table}

\begin{table*}[*location*] *text* \end{table*}

The optional argument [*location*] governs the order in which LaTeX attempts to fit the float into the document:

h (here) at the position in the text where the environment appear. In other words don't float (unless there is insufficient space on the rest of this page).

t (top) at the top of this or a following text page

b (bottom) at the bottom of this or a following page

p (page) on a separate page containing only floats

location can contain all four characters. The default is [tbp] which means that floats will be tried at the top of the page and then at the bottom if there is no space. If both these fail, LaTeX will accumulate floats until there are enough to make a *page of floats*.

7.3.1 Using the h command

When using the optional placement argument, be sure to give LaTeX plenty of room for manoeuvre. If you specify a series of [b] arguments in quick succession the floats may be spread out over successive pages, so some of your illustrations might end up a long way from where they are referenced in the text. It is a much better idea to use an argument of [htbp], which allows LaTeX to place the float at the top of the page if it cannot make space at the point in the text where the float environment appears. When a \clearpage or \cleardoublepage command (or the end of the document) is encountered, all floats are immediately output regardless of their placement options.

7.3.2 Problems with floats

The float mechanism does suffer from some bugs. If you have a large number of floats outstanding LaTeX can become confused and may put floats in the wrong order or on pages before they are referenced. The vertical layout of your document can be severely disrupted. The series of tables in Chapter 5 suffers from this problem and I had to take special action to persuade LaTeX to typeset them in the correct order. There are two workarounds to the problem. Firstly, try putting a [htbp] option on each float. LaTeX will then place many floats inline in the text, avoiding the build-up of unplaced floats that triggers the bug. If that fails, or produces output that does not suit your layout requirements then try issuing \clearpage commands to force output of floats.

7.3.3   Captions

Within a float environment the command \caption[*listtext*]{*text*} generates a caption using *text*. It also updates the current reference value (see page 104) to the number of the float so that a subsequent \label command can be used to access the figure or table number. The optional argument specifies the text to be used in the list of tables or list of figures. If absent, the caption text is used.

7.4   Handling graphics

TEX produces beautiful typeset output, but has few facilities for including graphics. This may be a historical defect — TEX was developed on large timesharing computers before personal computers and graphics workstations became so common. If you need pictures in your documents you have four options

1. Leave a blank space and paste the picture in after printing.

2. Leave a blank space and use a special DVI driver to include the picture when the document is printed. (This is just an electronic version of option 1.)

3. Let TEX build the picture out of dots, say by placing full stops.

4. Let TEX build the picture out of predefined characters, and supply a font that includes graphics primitives such as lines and curves.

7.4.1   Picture inclusion

Option 1 at least has the virtue of generality. Using the DVI driver to perform the same function presupposes that you have some way of preparing a drawing in machine-readable form and that your DVI driver is sophisticated enough to allow inclusion. There is a TEX command \special which allows DVI driver commands to be embedded in the DVI file, and you should read the manual for your DVI driver to see if suitable \special commands are available.

One disadvantage of both these options is that the fonts used for text within a drawing package are unlikely to be the same as TEX's fonts, leading to a visual mismatch between the text and the labels in a diagram. In addition, there is no universal standard for DVI driver commands. If you are intending to distribute your document to other people so that they can print it out themselves, then you had better avoid picture inclusion.

7.4.2   Pictures made up of dots

Building a picture out of dots is also general, and there is a macro package available called PICTEX that adopts this approach. In practice though this is far from satisfactory. TEX was designed to perform sophisticated text-oriented placement of relatively large character cells. It turns out that TEX usually only has to keep at most one and a half pages of text in memory at a time, and in fact its internal memory is quite small. It is very easy to exceed TEX's memory capacity when drawing even moderately complicated pictures using dots. Many TeX installations include a 'big' TeX which is a version of the TeX program recompiled with larger internal memory, but you may well find that the PICTeX approach is still unbearably slow. You will find advice on how to acquire PICTeX in Chapter 13.

7.4.3 Building pictures with special characters

LaTeX has a set of fonts that include line segments at various angles, arrows, curves and discs. They are accessed using special commands within a `picture` environment. Since the picture commands are limited to those graphical primitives represented in the special fonts, you can only draw simple objects. In particular, there are only a small number of available line angles and circle sizes.

The advantage of this approach is that LaTeX draws pictures by putting together relatively large characters, and this is much faster and consumes less memory than the same picture made up of dots.

7.5 The `picture` environment

A `picture` environment takes two parameters

```
\begin{picture}(width,height)(xoffset,yoffset)
putcommands
\end{picture}
```

Unusually, these parameters are delimited by parentheses. Such parameters are *coordinates* and they only appear within a `picture` environment. A coordinate is a comma-delimited pair of numbers with no explicit units. The coordinate units are set by the present value of the length register `\unitlength`. The default value is 1pt, but the entire picture can be scaled using a command of the form `\setlength{\unitlength}{2.5mm}`

width and *height* are the x and y dimensions of the picture on the page as multiples of `\unitlength`. Both numbers must be positive. The offset parameter is optional (even though it is not enclosed in square brackets) and sets the origin of the displayed picture. By default the bottom left corner will have coordinates (0,0). Example pictures with source code may be found at the end of the large example in Chapter 1 and in Figure 7.4 below.

Every graphics object has a *reference point* that is used to mark the position of the whole object. For boxes the reference point is the lower left corner. For lines and arrows, the reference point is the beginning of the line. For circles and discs and ovals, the reference point is at the centre.

7.5.1 `picture` commands

The only commands that may appear within a `picture` environment are declarations and *put* commands, which place graphics objects at specific coordinates. The available graphics objects are described in the next section.

\put(*coordinates*){*graphic-object*}

> places a single *graphic-object* with its reference point at the specified coordinates.

\multiput(*coordinates*)(*increments*){*repeat*}{*graphics-object*}

> puts *repeat* copies of *graphics-objects* starting at *coordinates* and offsetting each copy by *increments*.

The thickness of lines drawn in a `picture` environment have two standard values. The \thicklines and \thinlines declarations choose between them. The default is \thinlines. In addition, the thickness of horizontal and vertical lines (which are drawn using TₑX's `rule` commands) can be set to an arbitrary size using \linethickness{*length*}.

7.5.2   Graphics objects

LATₑX can draw boxes, lines, vectors, circles and discs (filled circles). In addition normal typeset text may be placed, although you must use a \parbox command to define the width of any paragraphs since by default the text is set in a single line.

7.5.3   Lines and vectors

\line(*slope*){*length*} and \vector(*slope*){*extent*} draw lines and lines with arrows (vectors). The slope values give the x and y steps for the line and must be in the range $-6 - - + 6$ for \line and $-4 - - + 4$ for \vector. In addition, the x and y fields must have a highest common divisor of 1, so (2,4) should be replaced by (1,2). *extent* specifies the maximum horizontal length of the line, unless its x-step is zero (i.e. a vertical line) in which case *extent* specifies the maximum vertical extent.

The line segments used to draw sloping lines are 10pt long, so the shortest sloping line that LATₑX can draw is 10pt long. Lines do *not* need to be multiples of 10pt long because LATₑX will overlap segments to get the correct length. If you ask for a line that is too short, nothing will be drawn. This restriction does not apply to horizontal and vertical lines because they are drawn using TₑX's `rule` commands which can handle any length and thickness.

7.5.4   Circles and discs

\circle{*extent*} draws a circle of diameter *extent* times \unitlength. The reference point is the centre of the circle. The *-form \circle*{*extent*} draws a disc. There are only a small set of available circle sizes going up to 40pt. The largest disc available is 15pt.

7.5.5   Joining curves and lines

The graphic fonts contain quarter circle symbols, and the \circle command makes a complete circle by setting four of these together. Quarter circles can also be used to make a smooth transition between straight lines.

\oval(*width,height*)[*part*] draws the largest oval (that is a rectangle with rounded corners) that can be contained in a rectangle of the specified *width* and *height*. The rounded corners will be formed using the largest possible circle segments. In general, the oval will be smaller then the requested size unless exactly the right sized circle segment is available.

The optional argument [*part*] can be used to limit the drawing to a half or quarter oval and comprises one or two of the following letters: l left, r right, t top and b bottom.

7.5.6   picture **boxes**

A picture box is a graphics object that can contain arbitrary LaTeX text. They are most commonly used for placing text labels in a picture.

> \makebox(*width,height*)[*position*]{*text*}
> \framebox(*width,height*)[*position*]{*text*}
> \dashbox{*dashlength*}(*width,height*)[*position*]{*text*}

These commands all make a box of dimensions (*width,height*) with reference point at the lower left corner. \framebox draws a solid box and \dashbox draws a box made up of dashes *dashlength* long. *dashlength* should be a common factor of *width* and *height* for tidy corners.

By default *text* is typeset horizontally and vertically centred. The optional *position* argument overrides this with one or two letters from: l flushleft, r flushright, t force to the top of the box and b force to the bottom.

The text is typeset as a single line, so if you want a paragraph you must use the \parbox command in the *text* parameter (see section 11.6). Note that if you subsequently scale the picture by changing the value of \unitlength that the labels will stay the same size.

A rectangular solid frame may be put round any graphics object with the command \frame{*graphics-object*}.

7.5.7   **Vertically aligned text**

Unfortunately, TeX is not able to rotate text, so unless you have a very unusual set of fonts you will not be able to make text labels that read from top to bottom. However, you can produce vertically aligned text, either by using a tabular environment, or with the command

> \shortstack[*format*]{*rows*}

which is almost an abbreviation for

> \begin{tabular}[b]{*format*} *rows* \end{tabular}

The \shortstack command does not leave space around it (which a tabular environment would). The command is illustrated in the large example in Chapter 1.

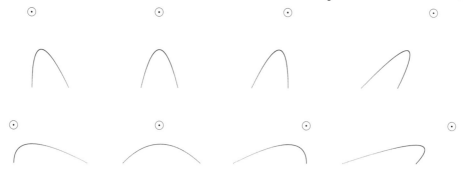

Figure 7.3 Sample Bezier curves

7.5.8   The `bezier` **curve drawing command**

Bezier curves are mathematical objects which can be used to draw sweeping curves that have guaranteed start and end points. They are useful for reproducing freehand drawings. LaTeX has a subsidiary style option called `bezier.sty` that you can incorporate into your documents in the usual way by supplying a [`bezier`] style option to your `\documentstyle` command. The option defines one new command:

`\bezier{`*count*`}(`*startx,starty*`)(`*controlx,controly*`)(`*finishx,finishy*`)`

which draws a second-order Bezier curve between the points (*startx, starty*) and (*finishx, finishy*) using a third point, (*controlx, controly*) to 'pull' the line into a curve. In general, the curve will *not* pass through the third point. The line will be marked with *count* dots spaced along its length.

Most people find it best to simply experiment with Bezier curves until they get the effect they want — some examples are shown in Figure 7.3. In each case the control point is marked with a ⊙ symbol.

7.5.9   **Pictures within pictures**

Typesetting pictures is time consuming. If you have a structure that is to be placed repeatedly, or used in more than one picture then it is more efficient to save it in a *savebox* (see section 11.6).

`\savebox{`*boxname*`}(`*width,height*`)[`*position*`]{`*text*`}` works in the same way as the `\makebox` command above, but produces no output, placing the result in box *boxname* which must have been previously declared using a `\newsavebox` command. A subsequent `\usebox{`*boxname*`}` command retrieves the contents of *boxname*.

Although `\savebox` commands save time when a picture is to be used repeatedly they do consume memory, which is rather limited in standard TeX implementations. The space is reclaimed when the scope region containing the `\savebox` is exited.

Figure 7.4 shows an example picture that exercises many of the features of the `picture` environment. The logic gates were drawn using Georg Horn's TeXcad program for MS-DOS which is described in Chapter 13, along with the Unix `xfig` program, both of which can produce LaTeX picture mode drawing commands ready

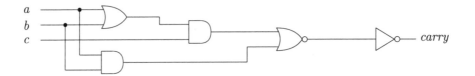

Figure 7.4 Example picture: logic gates

for inclusion in your document. The gates are designed to be used as \saveboxes: Bezier curves are especially demanding of memory and processor time, and considerable savings can be made if they are only constructed once.

```
\unitlength=1mm
\linethickness{0.4pt}
\newsavebox{\nore}
\savebox{\nore}(12,6){
\begin{picture}(12,6)
\bezier{60}(2,6)(7,6)(9,3)
\bezier{60}(2,0)(7,0)(9,3)
\bezier{50}(2,6)(4,3)(2,0)
\put(10.5,3){\line(1,0){1.5}}
\put(9.75,3){\circle{1.5}}
\put(0,5){\line(1,0){2.5}}
\put(0,1){\line(1,0){2.5}}
\end{picture}}

\newsavebox{\ande}
\savebox{\ande}(12,6){
\begin{picture}(12,6)
\put(0,1){\line(1,0){2}}
\put(5,0){\line(-1,0){3}}
\put(2,0){\line(0,1){6}}
\put(2,6){\line(1,0){3}}
\put(0,5){\line(1,0){2}}
\bezier{30}(5,0)(8,0)(8,3)
\bezier{30}(8,3)(8,6)(5,6)
\put(8,3){\line(1,0){4}}
\end{picture}}

\newsavebox{\ore}
\savebox{\ore}(12,6){
\begin{picture}(12,6)
\bezier{60}(2,6)(7,6)(9,3)
\bezier{60}(2,0)(7,0)(9,3)
\bezier{50}(2,6)(4,3)(2,0)
\put(9,3){\line(1,0){3}}
\put(0,5){\line(1,0){2.5}}
\put(0,1){\line(1,0){2.5}}
\end{picture}}
```

```
\begin{picture}(119,25)(0,100)
\put(10,120){\line(1,0){15}}
\put(25.00,115.00){\usebox{\ore}}
\put(10,116){\line(1,0){15}}
\put(25.00,103.00){\usebox{\ande}}
\put(10,112){\line(1,0){39}}
\put(21,108){\line(1,0){4}}
\put(17,104){\line(1,0){8}}
\put(49.00,111.00){\usebox{\ande}}
\put(37,118){\line(1,0){6}}
\put(43,118){\line(0,-1){2}}
\put(43,116){\line(1,0){6}}
\put(73.00,109.00){\usebox{\nore}}
\put(61,114){\line(1,0){12}}
\put(73,110){\line(-1,0){6}}
\put(67,110){\line(0,-1){4}}
\put(67,106){\line(-1,0){30}}
\put(85,112){\line(1,0){12}}
\put(6,120){\makebox(0,0)[cc]{\em a}}
\put(6,116){\makebox(0,0)[cc]{\em b}}
\put(6,112){\makebox(0,0)[cc]{\em c}}
\put(114,112){\makebox(0,0)[lc]
{\em carry}}
\put(21,120){\circle*{1}}
\put(17,116){\circle*{1}}
\put(21,108){\line(0,1){12}}
\put(17,104){\line(0,1){12}}
\put(97,112){\line(1,0){5}}
\put(102,109){\line(0,1){6}}
\put(102,115){\line(5,-3){5}}
\put(107,112){\line(-5,-3){5}}
\put(107.8,112){\circle{1.50}}
\put(108.50,112){\line(1,0){4.5}}
\end{picture}
\savebox{\nore{}} % to release memory
\savebox{\ande{}} % to release memory
\savebox{\ore{}} % to release memory
```

Figure 7.5 Example picture source code

8

Typesetting mathematics

Chapter 5 contains tables of maths mode characters including Greek, Calligraphic and special symbols. This chapter describes commands for putting these characters together into *formulae*.

Mathematics typesetting has its own set of rules and traditions. As well as requiring a huge variety of symbols, the *spacing* of formulae obeys special rules. TEX has a set of rules built in that is sufficient to cope with most engineering-level mathematics, and allows you to take complete control where necessary. The LaTeX maths commands do not exploit the full power of the underlying TEX commands, and if you are a professional mathematician or involved in typesetting particularly complex formula then you should consider obtaining $\mathcal{A}_{\mathcal{M}}\mathcal{S}$-LaTeX [Ame91], which provides the $\mathcal{A}_{\mathcal{M}}\mathcal{S}$-TEX advanced maths commands in a LaTeX style file. This chapter only describes the native LaTeX maths typesetting commands. For more information on TEX and $\mathcal{A}_{\mathcal{M}}\mathcal{S}$-TEX see the TEXbook [Knu86a] and Michael Spivak's *Joy of TEX*. $\mathcal{A}_{\mathcal{M}}\mathcal{S}$-LaTeX comes with its own manual as part of the distribution package.

When TEX is in maths mode it enforces its own spacing rules, so spaces in the input are simply discarded. Of course, spaces may still be required to delimit commands, so don't simply remove all space from your source file!

8.1 LaTeX maths mode environments

There are six LaTeX environments listed in Figure 8.1 that put TEX into maths mode. When typing the names of these environments, remember that English *maths* is American *math* and that LaTeX uses American spellings here as elsewhere.

An *in-text formula* is a sequence of maths mode symbols embedded in an ordinary paragraph. *Displayed formulae* are on set their own lines, indented and optionally numbered. The `displaymath` and `equation` environments produce one line formulae, usually centred. If necessary, they will split a formula across lines. In the `equation` environment, the equation number will be usually be typeset against the right margin. The subsidiary style option [`leqno`] moves the equation numbers to the left hand margin.

The `array` environment is just like the `tabular` environment described in Chapter 7 but the lines and the text in any @-expressions are typeset in maths mode. All the usual commands, including `\multicolumn`, `\cline` and `\hline` are available. Remember that the `tabular` and `array` environments yield a single box which can-

Name	Short form	use
math	\(...\) or $...$	in-text formula
displaymath	\[...\] or $$...$$	unnumbered displayed formula
equation		numbered displayed formula
array		matrix
eqnarray		numbered multiline equations
eqnarray*		nonnumbered multiline equations

Table 8.1 LATEX maths environments

not be split across pages. You will have to manually divide large arrays, just as you would large tables. It is possible to use an array as a component of an in-text formula, if for instance you wanted to set an entire matrix as a superscript. Figure 8.1 on page 85 shows an example of the `array` environment.

When showing the derivation of a result it is conventional to align the equations around the relation sign, optionally numbering the stages, which may be done with a three column `array` environment. This is such a common construction that LATEX provides the `eqnarray` environment as a shorthand. It is used just like a three column array, column 1 for the left hand side, the centre column for the relation and column three for the right hand side. An equation number is put on every line unless it includes a \nonumber command. The `eqnarray*` environment is identical to `eqnarray` except that all equation numbers are suppressed just as if every line contained a \nonumber.

8.2 Subscripts, superscripts and stacks

Superscripts $^{like\ this}$ are produced with the ^ command. Subscripts $_{like\ this}$ are produced with the _ command. As well as being vertically offset, subscripts and superscripts are set in smaller type.

You can superscript superscripts to produce expressions like x^{y+1^2} which was written as `$x^{{y+1}^2}$`. Note that the superscripts are strictly nested. Simply putting two superscripts in a row, such as `$x^{y+1}^2$` is an error. Supersuperscripts, and subsubscripts (not to say supersubscripts and subsuperscripts) are set in even smaller type. However the size reduction stops there — further levels of scripting will be set in the smallest type, otherwise you might need a magnifying glass to read the result.

The \prime character ′ is designed to be used in superscripts, so `$x^\prime$` produces x'.

\stackrel{*top*}{*bottom*} places *top* above *bottom* as a centrally placed superscript. It is often used with relations, as in

x\stackrel{\alpha}{\longrightarrow}y which produces $x \xrightarrow{\alpha} y$

8.3   Fractions and roots

A LATEX fraction is produced with \frac{*numerator*}{*denominator*}. The size of
the fraction will be adjusted for in-line formulae and displayed maths.

The command \sqrt[*root*]{*formula*} generates the nth root of *formula*. If the
optional argument is missing then the square root is printed

\sqrt[3]{x^2+y^2} gives $\sqrt[3]{x^2 + y^2}$

\sqrt{x^2+y^2} gives $\sqrt{x^2 + y^2}$

8.4   plain TEX fraction-like commands

plain has a variety of commands for building fraction-like formulae, and these
are also available in LATEX. The plain commands use an *infix* rather than a *pre-
fix* notation, so the commands appear like operators rather than commands with
parameters.

The plain equivalent to \frac is \over, so

$$x \text{ \over } y \text{ produces } \qquad \frac{x}{y},$$

which is the same as the output from \frac{x}{y}. The \atop command produces
a fraction with no fraction bar:

$$x \text{ \atop } y \text{ makes } \qquad \frac{x}{y}.$$

Finally, the binomial coefficients may be typeset using \choose which is just like
\atop except that the result is surrounded with parentheses:

$$x \text{ \choose } y \text{ produces } \qquad \binom{x}{y}.$$

Since these commands use an operator like notation you must use groups to nest
them.

8.5   Large delimiters

The delimiters shown in Table 5.18 will grow to surround any adjacent boxes when
prefaced by \left or \right. For instance

\[x=2\times (\sum^{15}_{i=1}
\frac{y_i}{y_{i+1}}) \]   produces

$$x = 2 \times (\sum_{i=1}^{15} \frac{y_i}{y_{i+1}})$$

but

```
\[x=2\times\left(\sum^{15}_{i=1}
\frac{y_i}{y_{i+1}}\right)\]       makes
```

$$x = 2 \times \left(\sum_{i=1}^{15} \frac{y_i}{y_{i+1}} \right)$$

The \left and \right commands must appear in pairs like \begin and \end, but the actual delimiters need not be paired. A \left or a \right followed by a full stop will typeset an invisible delimiter, fulfilling the requirement that delimiters be matched. This feature is often used for building *case* formulae:

```
\[x=\left\{ \begin{array}{ll}1&\mbox{if $y>0$}\\
                            0&\mbox{if $y\le0$}\\
\end{array} \right. \]
```

produces

$$x = \left\{ \begin{array}{ll} 1 & \text{if } y > 0 \\ 0 & \text{if } y \le 0 \end{array} \right.$$

8.5.1   The plain TEX cases command

The kind of relation shown above is such a common construction that plain TEX provides a special \cases command. This command is still available in LATEX, which underlines the fact that many of the commands described in the TEXbook may be used without modification in LATEX.

The plain command

```
\[x=\cases{1&\mbox{\rm if $y>0$}\cr
           0&\mbox{\rm if $y\le0$}\cr}\]
```

produces

$$x = \left\{ \begin{array}{ll} 1 & \text{if } y > 0 \\ 0 & \text{if } y \le 0 \end{array} \right.$$

There may be as many lines in the case command as you like and the left brace will expand as needed. Note that plain uses the \cr command where LATEX uses \\. The fields are separated by & characters, as in LATEX.

8.6   Ellipsis

A sequence or repeating pattern is usually indicated by a trail of dots... This kind of ellipsis in either text or maths mode can be produced by \ldots thus ... When you use ellipsis at the end of a sentence, you should ask for an inter-sentence space with \@ immediately afterwards (see section 5.3.4).

In mathematical typesetting three other forms of ellipsis are sometimes required

\cdots produces a string of *centred* centred dots: $\cdots$

$$P^{-1}AP = \begin{pmatrix} \lambda_1 & 0 & \cdots & 0 \\ 0 & \lambda_2 & \cdots & 0 \\ \vdots & \vdots & \ddots & \vdots \\ 0 & 0 & \cdots & \lambda_n \end{pmatrix}$$

```
\[
P^{-1}AP=\left(
\begin{array}{cccc}
\lambda_1&0    &\cdots&0\\
0    &\lambda_2&\cdots&0\\
\vdots&\vdots &\ddots&\vdots\\
0    &  &  0 &\cdots&\lambda_n\\
\end{array}
\right)
\]
```

Figure 8.1 Use of ellipsis

`\vdots` gives a vertical row of dots: $\vdots$

`\ddots` makes a diagonal row of dots: $\ddots$

The most common application of these forms is in the description of large matrices as shown in Figure 8.1.

8.7   Over and underlining

Over and underlining is to be discouraged in normal typeset text: use italic or bold type for emphasis instead.

In maths mode you can overline a formula, as well as putting braces above and below. Additionally, in maths and text mode you can underline text:

`\underline{Don't underline}` produces $\underline{\text{Don't underline}}$

`Read/$\overline{\rm Write}$` produces Read/$\overline{Write}$

8.8   Over and under braces

Similar commands will place braces under and over formulae:

`\overbrace{x_1+x_2+\cdots+x_{n-1}+x_{n}}`
produces
$$\overbrace{x_1 + x_2 + \cdots + x_{n-1} + x_n}$$

`\underbrace{x_1+x_2+\cdots+x_{n-1}+x_{n}}`
produces
$$\underbrace{x_1 + x_2 + \cdots + x_{n-1} + x_n}$$

If you subscript or superscript a brace then you will get a centred label, so

```
\underbrace{x_1+x_2+\cdots+x_{n-1}+x_{n}}_x
```
produces
$$\underbrace{x_1 + x_2 + \cdots + x_{n-1} + x_n}_{x}$$

8.9 Maths mode size styles

There are occasions when you might need to set a superscript in normal size text. Within maths mode there are four basic style declarations which mainly affect the size of text. The four styles, and their default uses are shown in Table 8.2, and they may be used within maths mode to change the size of text.

`\textstyle`	in-text formulae and items in the **array** environment
`\displaystyle`	displayed formulae
`\scriptstyle`	first level superscripts and subscripts
`\scriptscriptstyle`	higher-level subscripts and superscripts

Table 8.2 Maths text styles

`\textstyle` and `\displaystyle` are almost identical, using the same size characters in nearly all cases. However, `\textstyle` uses small versions of the symbols shown in Table 5.17 (such as $\int$) and places subscripts and superscripts for things like summation signs beside the operator as in $\sum_{i=1}^{n}$. This is done so that in-text formulae will not overlap adjoining lines. Displayed equations use the easier-to-read large forms from Table 5.17 since the vertical spacing can be adjusted to suit.

As you might expect, `\scriptstyle` and `\scriptscriptstyle` produce the small characters used for scripts and are analogous to the size changing commands for normal text described in Table 5.4.

8.10 Using text mode inside maths mode

The best way to insert some normal text into a formula is to place it into an hbox by using an `\mbox` command. TEX will automatically switch back into text mode within the box, but modes may be nested and their is nothing to stop you re-entering maths mode within the box. The LATEX case formula shown in section 8.5 above illustrates this technique.

8.11 Mixing bold and unbold maths

Chapter 5 described the `\boldmath` and `\unboldmath` commands which may be used to select heavy or normal weight maths characters. These declarations must be used in *text mode*, so if you want to mix bold and unbold maths you can use an `\mbox` command to nest into text mode, select the new character weight and then enter a nested maths mode:

LEFT	RIGHT ORD	OP	BIN	REL	OPEN	CLOSE	PUNCT	INNER
ORD	none	thin	med*	thick*	none	none	none	thin*
OP	thin	thin		thick*	none	none	none	thin*
BIN	med*	med*			med*			med*
REL	thick*	thick*		none	thick*	none	none	thick*
OPEN	none	none		none	none	none	none	none
CLOSE	none	thin	med*	thick*	none	none	none	thin*
PUNCT	thin*	thin*		thin*	med*	med*	thin*	thin*
INNER	thin*	thin	med*	thick*	med*	none	thin*	thin*

* except in subscripts, where none is used instead

Table 8.3 Maths spacing rules

```
\[\mbox{\boldmath $AM^{-1}$} = (0,1,\lambda)\]
```
gives

$$AM^{-1} = (0,1,\lambda)$$

8.12   Maths font loading

To conserve space, LaTeX only loads certain fonts when they are appear in the document. In text mode, LaTeX will quietly load any fonts it needs without bothering you, but if you try and use an unloaded font in maths mode you will get one of the following messages:

```
\scriptfont font-name is undefined
```

```
\scriptscriptfont font-name is undefined
```

```
\textfont font-name is undefined
```

If you get these messages, then insert the following command at the outermost level of your document (i.e. not inside a group or environment): `\load{size}{font}` where *size* is one of the size changing commands in Table 5.4 and *font* is one of the font selectors in Table 5.1. The command must appear before the first use of the font in maths mode — a good place for it would be in the preamble.

8.13   Spacing in maths mode

TeX uses a surprisingly simple set of rules to arrange the spacing within formulae. The tables of maths mode symbols in Chapter 5 identify a *type* for each symbol which will be one of

ORD ordinary formulae

OP enlargable operators

BIN binary operators

REL relations

OPEN opening delimiters

CLOSE closing delimiters

PUNCT punctuation

INNER a delimited formula

The result of a fraction command is of type INNER, most other formulae are of type ORD.

Table 8.3, adapted from the TEXbook shows the space that TEX inserts between two items of each type. The three spaces thin, med and thick refer to the space commands listed in section 5.3.2.

It should now be clear why there are three control sequences that all generate the | character on the page: sometimes a bar is used as a delimiter (the | command), sometimes as a relation (\mid) and sometimes as an ordinary component (\vert). You must select the correct sequence to get good spacing in your typeset output.

Sometimes TEX's rules are too simple and you need to insert some extra space. For instance, in the integral $\int x\,dx$, TEX has no way of knowing that there should be a small space before the dx, so you must explicitly insert one with $\int x\,dx$.

9

Cross referencing and bibliographies

Most large documents contain internal cross references and references to other papers and books. Maintenance of cross references is a tedious clerical procedure, in other words exactly the kind of thing that computers are good at. LaTeX allows you to insert a *label* at any point in a document. When a label is encountered, a note of the page and section in which the label occurred is made on an auxiliary file. Elsewhere in the document you may refer to the label, and the page or section number will be automatically inserted for you.

As in contents generation, the information on the auxiliary file is always one step behind because the information on the previous pass is inserted. If out-of-date information has been used then at the end of the run LaTeX issues the message

```
Label(s) may have changed.  Rerun to get cross references right.
```

It is possible for several runs to be needed before the cross references stabilise, so you must repeatedly run LaTeX until the message goes away.

Bibliographic references such as [Lam86] can also be constructed automatically by LaTeX. You can either keep all the reference information with the source file, or use external databases in association with the BibTeX programme to build bibliographies. If you write a lot of papers with bibliographies you will find that the BibTeX system can be used as the heart of a powerful on-line replacement for the more traditional card-index of literature references.

9.1 Defining labels

The command \label{*string*} makes an entry in the .aux file containing *string*, the page number on which this label was defined and the current *reference value*. *string* is an arbitrary string of characters with no embedded spaces. Within a document all label and bibliography *strings* must be unique or the error message

```
Label 'string' multiply defined
```

will be issued.

The reference value is set by the \refstepcounter command (see section 11.2.3). The following commands change the reference value

⋄ sectioning commands,

⋄ the `equation` environment which sets the reference value to the equation's number,

⋄ any theorem-like environment (of which `equation` is an example) defined using a \newtheorem command (see section 10.3),

⋄ the `eqnarray` environment which sets the reference value to the equation number of the line in the array, unless a \nonumber command has been issued,

⋄ \item commands in `enumerate` environments, which set the reference value to the item number,

⋄ \caption commands in `figure` and `table` environments which set the reference value to the figure or table number. Be sure to put \label commands *after* the \caption command or inside the argument, since it is the \caption command that changes the reference value, not the environment!

⋄ direct use of the \refstepcounter command.

9.2   Referencing labels

The page number of a label is retrieved with \pageref{*string*} where *string* is the same text string used in the \label command. The reference value of label is retrieved using the \ref{*string*} command.

```
This is section~\ref{tag} on page~\pageref{tag}.
\label{tag}
```

produces

This is section 9.2 on page 90.

Note the use of the tie before the \ref command to stop line breaking.

9.3   Referencing citations

The command \cite{*string*} prints a *citation*. *string* must be defined in an external bibliography (bbl) file created by BibTeX or in a `thebibliography` environment. *string* may not contain a comma. The exact form of the printed citation depends on the bibliography style in use.

You can combine multiple citations by using a comma delimited list of *string*s as in

```
\cite{latexbook,texbook}
```

which produces

[Lam86, Knu86a]

There should not be any spaces between the *string* arguments.

An optional argument to the cite command allows text to be included as part of the printed citation.

```
\cite[the \LaTeX\ book]{latexbook}
```

produces

[Lam86, the LaTeX book]

The command `\nocite{`*string1,string2,...*`}` causes the citations for *string1, string2,...* to be added to the bibliography listing without a citation actually appearing in the text.

9.4 Defining citations using `thebibliography`

The environment `thebibliography` is used when you want a document to be completely self contained rather than using BibTeX and an external database file.

`\begin{thebibliography}{`*longestlabel*`}` *citations* `\end{thebibliography}`

acts like a `list` environment where each item is a single citation. *longestlabel* is a text string used to specify the formatting of the list. It should be at least as long as the longest item label in the list.

Each citation begins with the command `\bibitem[`*biblabel*`]{`*string*`}`. The *string* is the citation key used by the matching `\cite` command. If the optional argument *biblabel* is present, then it is used as the list label, otherwise a number is used generated with the `enumi` counter. When a `\cite` command is used, the label is inserted at the point of the citation.

9.5 Defining citations using an external database file

The `\cite{`*string*`}` command makes a note on the `.aux` file of *string*. These entries can be read by an auxiliary program called BibTeX that will extract the relevant entries from a database file and write a bibliography file (of filetype `bbl`) that contains a suitable `thebibliography` environment for insertion in the parent document.

The command `\bibliography{`*bibliographyfiles*`}` makes a note in the `.aux` file of *bibliographyfiles* which is a comma delimited list of external bibliography database files. These files conventionally have the filetype `.bib`. Their format is described below. The command also includes the most recent `bbl` file should contain a `thebibliography` environment generated by the BibTeX program.

9.6 Changing the style of automatically generated bibliographies

If you use the explicit `thebibliography` environment you can specify the ordering of entries and their labels directly. BibTeX uses a system of *bibliography styles* analogous to the LaTeX styles to specify the formatting and ordering of bibliography

```
>bib lbook

This is BibTeX, Version 0.99c

The top-level auxiliary file: LBOOK.aux

The style file: alpha.bst

Database file #1: adrian.bib
```

Figure 9.1 Screen output of the BibTeX program

entries. You specify the style with a `\bibliographystyle{style}` command where
style may be

> unsrt entries in order of appearance in the text and are labelled by
> numbers, e.g.[12]

> plain entries sorted alphabetically by author and labelled with numbers

> abbrv entries sorted alphabetically by author and labelled with num-
> bers, with some parts abbreviated

> alpha entries sorted alphabetically by author and labelled with the first
> three characters of the author's name and the year of publication,
> e.g. [Joh90]

9.7   Running BibTeX

You must run LaTeX on your document at least once to generate an `.aux` file. Your
source file should contain a `\bibliographystyle` command specifying one of the
styles above or a locally produced style. It must also contain a `\bibliography`
command specifying one or more `bib` files. The relevant commands for this book
which are used to produce the bibliography at the back are

```
\bibliographystyle{alpha}
\bibliography{adrian}
```

You run BibTeX by issuing the command `bibtex filename` where filename is
the name of the parent document file. Figure 9.1 shows part of the BibTeX screen
output when run on this book. Figure 9.2 shows part of the `bbl` file produced,
which is a single `thebibliography` environment ready for inclusion in the parent
file.

Note that every time you add or remove citations from your document you must
run BibTeX again to regenerate the bibliography. I once had to shorten a paper for
publication and forgot to rerun BibTeX with the result that the editor complained
that I had twice as many references as were actually cited in the text!

```
\begin{thebibliography}{Lam86}

\bibitem[ISO80]{pascal:standard}
ISO.
\newblock {\em {Second DP 7185---Specification for the
  Computer Programming Language Pascal}}.
\newblock International Standards Organisation, 1980.

\bibitem[Knu84]{texbook}
Donald~E. Knuth.
\newblock {\em {The \TeX book}}.
\newblock Addison Wesley, 1984.

\bibitem[Lam86]{latexbook}
L.~Lamport.
\newblock {\em {\LaTeX\ user's guide \& reference manual}}.
\newblock Addison Wesley, 1986.

\end{thebibliography}
```

Figure 9.2 bbl file output of the B<small>IB</small>T_EX program

9.8   The format of bib files

By way of a first example Figure 9.3 shows the bib file entries that were used to produce the bibliography for this book.

All bibfile entries are of the form

>   @*documenttype*{*string,fields*}

documenttype specifies the type of the document which governs the kind of information reproduced in the bibliography. For instance a journal article usually has an entry for the month of publication, whereas a book would not. The available document types are summarised in Table 9.1.

string is the text string used in the corresponding \cite commands.

fields is a comma delimited list of field entries, each of the form

>   *fieldname* = *fieldtext*

where *fieldname* may be selected from those in Table 9.2. For each document type there is a set of required and a set of optional fields defined for the standard styles. You will get an error message if you omit a required field. Optional fields will be used if present, but may be omitted if inappropriate or if you do not have the necessary information. Any other field types are ignored, so it is possible to put arbitrary information into the bib file simply by using field names that are unused by the style files. A popular choice is to add an **abstract** field to the entry.

```
@book{latexbook,
author="Lamport, L.",
title="{\LaTeX\ user's guide \& reference manual}",
publisher = "Addison Wesley",
year="1986"}

@book{texbook,
author="Knuth, Donald E.",
title="{The \TeX book}",
publisher = "Addison Wesley",
year="1984"}

@book{pascal:standard,
        author="ISO",
        title="{Second DP 7185---Specification for the
        Computer Programming Language Pascal}",
        publisher = "International Standards Organisation",
        year="1980"}
```

Figure 9.3 bib file format

article	journal paper or magazine article
book	published book
booklet	as for book but without a publisher
inbook	part of a book(typically a chapter)
incollection	part of a book with its own title
inproceedings or conference	conference paper
manual	technical manual
mastersthesis	
misc	anything else
phdthesis	
proceedings	conference proceedings
techreport	technical report
unpublished	

Table 9.1 bib file document entry types

address	publisher's address
annote	annotation (not used by standard bibliography styles).
author	author's name(s). See section 9.8.2.
booktitle	title of a book. See section 9.8.1.
chapter	chapter number
edition	book edition
editor	editor's name(s). See section 9.8.2.
howpublished	for documents published inhouse, or in other unusual ways.
institution	name of institutional publisher
journal	journal name (may be abbreviated).
key	sort field if no author or editor
month	month of publication
note	any additional information for insertion in the bibliography
number	number of a journal or technical report
organization	sponsoring organisation for a conference
pages	list of page numbers or ranges
publisher	publisher's name
school	University school
series	name of an entire series of books
title	See section 9.8.1
type	type of a technical report
volume	volume number
year	year of publication

Table 9.2 BibTeX field names

fieldtext is a text string containing no unbalanced { or } characters surrounded by double quote characters (") or braces[1].

9.8.1 Typing titles

Some bibliography styles capitalise titles, and some use lower case. In practice the style will either print the title field exactly as it is written in the bib file or it will force all but the first letter to lowercase. As a result, you should type titles exactly as they would be if they were capitalised, and let the bibliography style decide whether to use lower case.

9.8.2 Typing names

A bibliography style decides whether to use full first names or initials and whether the second or first names should appear first. You must include as much information as possible so do not use initials in the bib file unless you do not know the full name.

A BibTeX author or editor field comprises a series of names separated by the word **and**. If there are too many authors to appear in a conventional bibliography

---

[1]If the text string is a string of digits then the enclosing quotes or braces may be omitted.

the list is terminated by the words **and others**. The bibliography styles convert this to *et al.*

A simple name is typed as it reads **John Smith**. If you include middle names **John James Smith** then the bibliography style will usually initialise it if it is capitalised, otherwise it assumes that it is an auxiliary word and reproduces it in full, as in **John de Smith**. This causes a problem with some names that comprise multiple capitalised words as do some foreign names or double-barrelled names without a hyphen. In that case use the last name, first name convention — **Smythe Thompson, Reginald**.

Braces may be used to enclose text that is to be treated literally, for instance a name containing the word **and** or a comma which would otherwise be parsed using the rules above. This is most likely to be a problem with commercial names such as **Sue, Grabbit and Run, Solicitors**.

9.8.3   Abbreviations in the bib file

Abbreviations may be defined by the bibliography style or in the `.bib` file. An abbreviation is a string of characters with no embedded spaces or any occurrence of the following characters: " # % ' ( ) , = { }.

You define abbreviation using a pseudo document name of **string**, so the entry

```
@string{short = "replacement for a long string of authors"}
```

allows you to subsequently use an entry of the form

```
author=short
```

An abbreviation defined in the bibliography file takes precedence over one defined in the style file.

9.9   Distributing bibliographies

If you send your document to other people you must either send them a copy of your `.bib` files, or send them the output of the BibTeX run. The best way to do this is to use BibTeX while you are writing your document, but then remove the \bibliography command from the document file and insert the contents of the `.bbl` file at the same point. This will ensure that anybody can just run your document through LaTeX even if they do not have, or do not know how to use BibTeX.

10

Defining commands

LaTeX allows you to define new commands as abbreviations for frequently used command sequences, or even redefine existing commands so as to change LaTeX's normal behaviour. This chapter shows how to define and redefine commands, environments and theorem-like environments, which have clauses numbered in sequence throughout a document.

10.1 Making new commands

The command

$\qquad$ \newcommand{\ *commandname*}{*definition*}

associates *definition* with the control sequence \commandname, so that every occurrence of \commandname will be replaced by the text *definition*, so for example

$\qquad$ \newcommand{\th}{th}

defines a command \th that may be used in dates, so that

$\qquad$ Wednesday 17\th\ October produces Wednesday 17th October.

Whenever you find a piece of text appearing frequently you should define a command for it as an abbreviation.

When LaTeX encounters a command that has been defined in this way, it replaces it with the contents of the *definition* parameter. The outermost braces are stripped off, so if you want to declare a local scope you must use another set of braces within the parameter.

10.1.1 New commands with parameters

One, or several pieces of text may be supplied to a command when it is called. As for predefined commands, the parameters are enclosed in braces (see section 2.1.6). An optional argument to \newcommand specifies the number of parameters to expect. Within the text of each command, the first parameter is represented by #1, the second by #2 and so on.

$\qquad$ \newcommand{\comb}[2]{$^{#1}$C$_{#2}$}

defines a command with two parameters, so that

$\qquad$ \comb{4}{6} then produces $^{4}C_{6}$

10.1.2   Redefining existing commands

It could be disastrous if you accidentally redefined an existing command. This is easy to do since there are some commands that are internal to LATEX and are not documented in this book. As a check against this, LATEX refuses to change the definition of a command that already exists and issues an error message.

Sometimes you really do want to redefine an existing command, in which case use the command

> `\renewcommand{\`*commandname*`}{`*definition*`}`

which works exactly like `\newcommand`, except that `\`*commandname* must already exist. You will find examples of command definition and redefinition in the next two chapters

10.2   Environments

An environment is really a pair of commands, the `\begin` part which sets up new formatting parameters, and the `\end` part which restores previous behaviour. You can define your own environments using `\newenvironment` and `\renewenvironment`:

> `\newenvironmnent{`*environment name*`}{`*begintext*`}{`*endtext*`}`

defines a new environment. Most often new environments are modifications to existing environments. For instance a document might require important warnings to be set out as a display using bold type with the word warning centred above:

```
\newenvironment{warn}%
{\begin{quote}\begin{center}{\bf Warning}\end{center}\\[2ex]}%
{\end{quote}}
%
\begin{warn}
If you switch the machine off while the disk activity light is
on, you may suffer data loss or corruption. Wait for disk
activity to cease before removing power.
\end{warn}
```

produces

Warning

> If you switch the machine off while the disk activity light is on, you may suffer data loss or corruption. Wait for disk activity to cease before removing power.

Note the use of the line terminated by %. You will recall from section 2.1.6 that there must be no white space separating a command and its parameters. Normally a new line is treated a whitespace, and so simply putting the parameters on separate lines would generate an error. Terminating a line with a comment causes the rest of the line *including the newline* to be discarded.

As before, use `\renewenvironment` to redefine an existing environment so as to avoid accidental disruption of LATEX's operation.

Proposition 1 *The first proposition*

Intervening text

Proposition 2 *The second proposition*

```
\newtheorem{prop}{Proposition}
\begin{prop}
The first proposition
\end{prop}
Intervening text
\begin{prop}
The second proposition
\end{prop}
```

Figure 10.1 Numbered environments (theorems)

10.3   Counted environments

There are environments such as `equation` that have an associated counter. Each use of the environment increments the value of the counter[1]. You can declare a counted environment using

> `\newtheorem{`*name*`}{`*caption*`}[`*enclosing-counter*`]`

The behaviour of a numbered environment is illustrated in Figure 10.1. Each environment body is preceded by the *title* parameter and a number set in bold type.

If the optional *enclosing-counter* parameter is present, then the theorem counter will be reset to one each time the enclosing counter is stepped. This is usually used to start a new sequence of theorem numbers for each chapter or section. You will find more information on enclosed counters in section 11.2 in the next chapter.

10.3.1   Sharing counters

A variant on the `\newtheorem` command may be used to make two environments share the same counter:

> `\newtheorem{`*name*`}[`*shared-counter*`]{`*title*`}`

In this case the optional parameter specifies an already defined numbered environment. Both that environment and the new environment will share a counter, so that they will be numbered in the same sequence.

---

[1]The LaTeX book calls these 'theorem-like environments'

11

LATEX style parameters

This chapter is about *visual formatting*, or the direct specification of text placement. As has been stressed throughout, the whole point of LATEX is that you should write your text without considering the layout on the page, using generic commands like \section and \caption. The actual typescript for these commands is defined in the style file, not in your document However, there will come a time when you wish to change the standard style files. Fortunately, it is not always necessary to write a complete new file because LATEX has a large number of *style parameters* that are directly accessible to you from within a document, and you can use these to make minor modifications to the layout.

A simple example is the command \labelitemi which is used to generate the mark in an itemize environment. By default, \labelitemi is defined to be \bullet, but this can be overridden with an optional parameter to the \item command within an itemize environment. If you need to do this more than once or twice then you can instead redefine \labelitemi. I rather prefer diamonds (⋄) to bullets, so in the preamble for most of my documents I say

```
\renewcommand{\labelitemi}{$\diamond$},
```

giving itemised lists like that on page 23.

You will recall from Chapter 2 that TEX has six kinds of registers. The first part of this chapter is about the details of register operations and arithmetic. Following that is a series of annotated diagrams that show you which parameters affect spacing and layout for pages, lists, floats, marginal notes and so on. This chapter does not describe LATEX programming or how to redefine formatted text items like section headings and captions which require non-trivial modifications to the style file. The next chapter analyses the contents of the standard styles, and with its help you will be able to produce completely new style files, and exercise much of the full power of the underlying TEX language.

11.1 LATEX variables revisited

In section 2.4 the six types of TEX variable were listed — counters, lengths, boxes, token lists, skip registers and maths skip registers. Counters hold integers (whole numbers), lengths hold distances, boxes hold typeset pieces of text that are snapshots of parts of a page, token lists hold strings of TEX commands and the two kinds of skips hold the *glue* or springs that are used to pad out the words and lines on a page. Very loosely speaking, skips correspond to the white space on the typeset page.

TeX only has space for 256 registers of each class, and in LaTeX many of these are already in use, so you must be restrained in your use of counter and length registers.

LaTeX provides facilities for defining and manipulating counters, lengths and boxes, and also allows you to insert glue, although not to declare glue registers. It *is* possible to use the more arcane kinds of registers, such as token lists, since the full set of TeX primitives is always available, but it is unwise to do this unless you are a seasoned TeX programmer because it is easy to upset LaTeX by going behind its back. Some hints on TeX programming in its full glory will be found in the next chapter, but serious aspiring programmers would be well advised to acquire some of the books listed in the introduction to Chapter 12.

11.2   Counters

A counter is a register that holds a single integer. The page number and the present chapter, section and subsection numbers are held in independent counters called page, chapter, section and so on. Counters can exist in a hierarchy, that is counter A might *enclose* counter B in which case B will be reset to zero every time A is incremented. The LaTeX \chapter and sectioning commands use this facility to ensure that, say, the section number goes back to zero at the start of a new chapter.

11.2.1   Declaring counters and printing their values

You can declare a new counter with the command

        \newcounter{*countername*}[*enclosing counter*]

This creates a new counter called *countername* which must be a previously undefined string of characters. The counter name is *not* a control word, so there must be no leading \. Hence dayofmonth is a valid LaTeX counter name but \dayofmonth is not. The optional argument [*enclosing counter*] names an *already defined* counter that encloses the new counter. Whenever the enclosing counter is stepped *countername* will be zeroed.

When a counter is created, it is initialised to zero and LaTeX automatically defines a command named \the*countername* which will print the contents of the counter as an Arabic numeral.

The \the*countername* command is in fact defined by LaTeX to be an abbreviation for \arabic{*countername*}. \arabic is one of six counter printing commands, and you can redefine \the*countername* to use any of them:

        \arabic{*countername*} arabic numerals

        \roman{*countername*} lower case Roman numerals

        \Roman{*countername*} upper case Roman numerals

\alph{*countername*} lower case letters a through z. The value must be in the range 1–26.

\Alph{*countername*} upper case letters A through Z. The value must be in the range 1–26.

\fnsymbol{*countername*} a symbol from the following sequence which are used for footnotes on title pages. The value must be in the range 1–9, and \fnsymbol may only be used in maths mode.

$$* \quad \dagger \quad \ddagger \quad \S \quad \P \quad \| \quad ** \quad \dagger\dagger \quad \ddagger\ddagger$$

11.2.2   More on page numbering

The \pagenumbering command simply redefines the command \thepage to change the way the page counter is typeset. You can achieve more complicated effects by, for example:

```
\renewcommand{\thepage}{\fbox{\Roman{page}}}   \thepage
```

which produces

$$\boxed{\text{CIII}}$$

If you redefine one of the predefined counters like this, then the new definition will be used by LaTeX whenever it needs to print the counter too, so after executing the \renewcommand{\thepage}... all the page numbers will be printed using a boxed Roman numeral. Conventionally, the top matter of a book, such as the preface and table of contents is numbered using lower case Roman numerals, and Arabic page numbering starts at the first page of Chapter 1. You can get this sort of effect by inserting \renewcommand{\thepage}{\roman{page}} at the start of your document and then \renewcommand{\thepage}{\arabic{page} immediately after the first \chapter command. The definition of \thepage used to produce a page number is the one in effect just as the page is cut, so putting the \renewcommand immediately after the \chapter command (which starts a new page) will ensure that the previous page is correctly numbered.

11.2.3   LaTeX commands to manipulate counter values

LaTeX allows you to add (possibly negative) numbers to counters. More general arithmetic (although not *much* more general) is possible using the TeX commands described in the next section. The following commands may be used to change the value of a counter

\setcounter{*countername*}{*number*}
   set the value of *countername* to *number*

\addtocounter{*countername*}{*number*}
   increment the value of *countername* by *number*

\stepcounter{*countername*}

> increment *countername* by one and zero any counters that are enclosed by it.

\refstepcounter{*countername*}

> increment *countername* by one, zero any counters that are enclosed by it and update the present *reference value*. The reference value is a counter that is used by the \label command. Whenever a \label command is encountered, LATEX makes a note of the pagenumber and current reference value, so that you can refer to them using the \ref and \pageref commands. The sectioning and \caption commands set the reference value automatically. You might use \refstepcounter in theorem and other environments to give a reference number.

In the above commands *number* may either be a literal positive or negative integer or \value{*countername*}, which returns the number held in *countername* in a form usable by the printing commands. The name of a counter itself does not return its value as in most programming languages, so \setcounter{mycounter}{chapter} is an error and you must use \setcounter{mycounter}{\value{chapter}} instead.

Both literal numbers and \value commands may be preceded by + or - signs to modify the sign. Each preceding - multiplies the number by -1, so +---+--6 is the same as -6.

TEX understands decimal, octal, hexadecimal and ASCII literal numbers. The following are all valid ways of loading the decimal number 78_{10} into mycounter:

```
\setcounter{mycounter}{78}       %decimal
\setcounter{mycounter}{"4E}      %hexadecimal
\setcounter{mycounter}{'116}     %octal
\setcounter{mycounter}{`N}       %ASCII character
\setcounter{mycounter}{`\N}      %ASCII control symbol
```

As you might expect, octal constants must only contain the digits 0–7 and hexadecimal constants the digits 0–9 along with the letters A–F. The ASCII character constants comprise a backquote character ` followed by either an ASCII character or a control sequence made up of a \ followed by an ASCII character. This is necessary because special characters like % would be given their special meaning unless they are preceded by \, so

```
\setcounter{mycounter}{'%}
```

would be interpreted as most of a \setcounter command followed by a comment, and TEX would look on the next line for the rest of the command.

11.2.4   TEX counter arithmetic commands

By using TEX commands you can multiply and divide the contents of counters as well as just add and subtract. You need to refer to the counters as \value{*counter*} rather than using the LATEX name directly, which TEX will not understand.

```
\newcounter{mycounter}\themycounter\\                                      0
\setcounter{mycounter}{6}\themycounter\\                                   6
\setcounter{mycounter}{\value{page}}\themycounter\\                        105
\addtocounter{mycounter}{-\value{page}}\themycounter\\                     0

\value{mycounter} \value{page} \themycounter\\   %Horrible                 105
\advance \value{mycounter} by -\value{page} \themycounter\\                0
\value{mycounter} = 6 \themycounter\\                                      6

\multiply \value{mycounter} by 2 \themycounter\\                           12
\divide \value{mycounter} by 3 \themycounter\\                             4
\divide \value{mycounter} by -5 \themycounter                              0
```

Figure 11.1 LaTeX and TeX counter arithmetic

You can assign values to a counter, add, multiply and divide using these commands:

> \value{*counter*} = *number*
>> assign *number* to *counter*

> \advance \value{*counter*} by *number*
>> add *number* (which may be negative for subtraction) to *counter*.

> \multiply \value{*counter*} by *number*
>> multiply *counter* by *number*. Be careful not to overflow the range of a counter which is from -2^{31} to $+2^{31}$, or ± 2147483647.

> \divide \value{*counter*} by *number*
>> divide *counter* by *number*. Since counters are integer variables, only the integer part of the result is kept and the remainder is discarded. Division by zero is, of course, illegal.

In fact the assignment symbol = and the keyword by are optional in the above, and you may sometimes see TeX commands of the form

> \value{mycounter}\value{anothercounter}

which copies the contents of anothercounter into mycounter. The wise TeX user will realise that TeX source code can be difficult enough to read without resorting to this kind of abbreviation, and I strongly advise you to always insert the keywords.

These commands and some of the LaTeX commands are illustrated in Figure 11.1. The output from this sequence of commands is shown on the right. Counter assignment and addition are illustrated using both LaTeX and TeX commands, followed by multiplication and division.

11.3   Lengths

A *length* is a register that holds a distance value, such as \textwidth which specifies the width of text on a page. Superficially a length looks like a counter but a length is allowed to have a fractional part (i.e. it may be a real number) and literal lengths must have an accompanying unit of measure.

11.3.1 Declaring length registers

You can make your own length registers with the \newlength{*lengthregister*} command where *lengthregister* is a control word not previously defined. Note that the name of a length register *does* have a preceding \, unlike the name of counter. The value of the length register is initialised to zero when declared.

11.3.2 LᴬTᴇX length register commands

The contents of a length register can be changed using the following commands which are analogous to the counter changing commands

\setlength{*lengthregister*}{*length*}
> sets the *lengthregister* to *length*

\addtolength{*lengthregister*}{*length*}
> increments *lengthregister* by *length*

\settowidth{*lengthregister*}{*text*}
> *text* is typeset on a a single line and then *lengthregister* is set to the length of that line. No output is generated (i.e. the typeset line is discarded).

The *length* parameter in the above commands may be either the name of another length register, or a *literal length*.

A literal length is an optional sign followed by a positive or negative integer followed by an optional decimal point (denoted by . or ,) and another positive integer followed by a length unit chosen from the list shown in Table 11.1. Hence 72.27pt and 1in both represent the same distance. Lengths can be negative: when used in spacing commands such as \hspace and \vspace positive lengths move to the right or down the page, and negative lengths to the left or up the page.

The point and pica are typesetters' units. A didot point dd is slightly larger than an English point, and is used in some continental countries. The cc is thus the European analogue of the pica.

The scaled point sp is TᴇX's internal unit of measure, and mainly appears when converting lengths to integer values for the purpose of loading into counters (see section 11.5 below). TᴇX does not internally handle real numbers, and when a length with a decimal point in it is read in it is multiplied up and stored as a 32-bit two's complement integer. This is done because, whilst 32-bit integer arithmetic is reliably portable across different computers, real number arithmetic may produce slightly different answers on different machines, and a fundamental design goal of TᴇX was to produce identical typeset output on a variety of machines. The largest distance that can be represented in TᴇX is $2^{30} - 1$sp or about 5.75 metres. The smallest distance is 1sp, or about 0.01 wavelengths of light [Knu86a].

The rather strange units em and ex are font specific dimensions. Traditionally an em is the width of a capital M and an ex the height of a lower case x. In practice,

mm	millimetre
cm	centimetre
in	inch
pt	point (there are 72.27 points to the inch)
bp	big point (there are 72 big points to the inch)
pc	pica (one pica is 12pt)
dd	didot point (1dd is $\frac{1238}{1157}$pt)
cc	cicero (there are 12cc in one dd)
sp	scaled point (there are 65536sp in 1pt)
em	roughly, the *width* of an M in the current font
ex	roughly, the *height* of an x in the current font

Table 11.1 Length dimensional units

modern fonts do not necessarily conform to these conventions, but nevertheless every TEX font will have these two associated lengths which are characteristic of the vertical and horizontal spreads of the characters. Spacing parameters within the text should usually be expressed in terms of the em and ex units so that they will automatically adjust to changes in font. Heights (such as interparagraph spacing) should be measured in exes and widths (such as paragraph indentation) measured in ems.

11.3.3 TEX commands for manipulating lengths

All of the TEX arithmetic commands described in section 11.2.4 may be used with length registers as well, with the proviso that literal lengths must have a unit of measure, and may have a fractional part after the decimal point. The octal, hexadecimal and character constant notations may be used to represent integer lengths too, so 'Hbp is a valid length, equal to 1in since H is ASCII 72, and there are 72 bp to the inch.

The LATEX name of a length register *is* the same as the TEX name (unlike the case with counters) so you can directly use the name and must not use the \value command. Hence for counters

```
\newcounter{mycounter}\value{mycounter}=-16
```

but for lengths

```
\newlength{\mylength}\mylength=-16.00pt
```

Note that the length name has a leading \ and the literal length has a decimal part and a unit.

As a final twist, it turns out that the numeric part of a number may be empty, so you may see the following bizarre constructions in other people's TEX code (but please, never your own)

```
\mylength.in      or even      \mylength,in
```

These both set `\mylength` to zero points. The = keyword has been omitted, as have both of the numeric parts of the literal number, so all that is left is a length register name, a decimal point and a unit keyword.

11.4   Rubber lengths and skips

In TEX terminology, a *skip* or glue item is a stretchable distance that is used to space out the typeset text. In the LATEX book, skips are called rubber lengths. Rubber lengths have a *natural length* which is just like a dimension. Left to themselves, skips will behave like spaces of their natural length. However, each skip also has a shrinkability and an expandability. A rubber length is written as

dimension plus *dimension* minus *dimension*

so each skip is really three dimensions coupled together. In fact the `plus` and `minus` clauses are both optional and if you leave them out then they default to 0pt.

The skip `23pt plus 5pt minus 1pt` has a natural length of 23pt, but will shrink to 22pt or expand to 28pt if necessary. The skip `23pt plus 1pt` will expand to 24pt but will not shrink at all. So really, a skip specifies a *range* of lengths with a preferred value. The `plus` and `minus` symbols are keywords like `pt` and `mm`, and like all keywords are only interpreted in certain contexts, in this case anywhere a literal skip is expected.

The stretch and shrink values come into play when TEX is attempting to find good line or page breaks. After splitting a paragraph up into lines of roughly the same length TEX squeezes or pulls the words until the ends of the line meet the left and right margins. Sometimes TEX cannot squeeze the glue sufficiently, in which case you get an `Overfull \hbox ...` warning message and TEX lets the text hang out into the right hand margin. If you ask for some unusual formatting you may get into the situation where TEX cannot stretch the glue enough either, in which case you get an `Underfull \hbox...` message. The typeset line will contain too much whitespace, or be *loose* in printers' parlance.

11.4.1   Using skips in LATEX

LATEX provides very little direct support for skips for the simple reason that the interline and interword spacings should be a property of the *style* not the document. If you want to insert some space, just use the horizontal and vertical spacing commands such as `\vspace` and `\bigskip` described in section 5.3.2. You will probably never need to define skip or maths skip registers and so LATEX does not provide any commands to do so. I have discussed skips in some detail here because you will need to understand them when you come to write your own style files.

text	`\hspace{\fill}text\hspace{\fill}`
text	`\hspace{\stretch{1}}text\hspace{\fill}`
text	`\hspace{\stretch{1}}text\hspace{\stretch{1}}`
text	`\hspace{\stretch{1}}text\hspace{\stretch{2}}`
text	`\hspace{\stretch{1}}text\hspace{\stretch{3}}`

Figure 11.2 Inserting spring commands

11.4.2   Infinitely stretchable glue

Sometimes it is useful to be able to tell TEX just to use as much glue as it needs. There is a special dimension keyword `fill` which really means infinite. So a skip of `0pt plus 1fill` means insert a spring that can stretch to any length.

LATEX does provide predefined infinite skips. The command word `\fill` expands to `0pt plus 1fill` and may be used as a parameter to the `\hspace` and `\vspace` commands. Fills left or right justify text, and text between two fills will be centred.

It turns out to be useful to have fills with different stretchabilities. The standard stretchable value is denoted by `\fill`. The `\stretch{multiplier}` command gives a fill with stretchability *multiplier* times that of a `\fill`, so that `\stretch{1}` is a synonym for `\fill`. `\stretch` may be used to place text at an arbitrary position between boundaries, by inserting springs with different stretchiness on either side. The ratio of whitespace on each side of the text will be the ratio of the stretchiness of the springs. These effects are illustrated in Figure 11.2 for horizontal spacing using `\hspace{\fill}` commands, and similar vertical effect may be obtained with `\vspace{\fill}` commands.

11.5   Interchanging skips, lengths and counters

A skip is three dimensions defining a range, and a dimension is really an integer number of scaled points. You can supply a skip when TEX is just expecting a length, and the expand and shrink values will simply be discarded. Similarly, you can supply a length when TEX is expecting an integer and TEX will use the equivalent number of scaled points. So,

```
\newlength{\mylength}\newcounter{mycounter}
\mylength=10pt plus 3pt minus 0pt
\value{mycounter}=\mylength
```

sets `\mylength` to 10pt, and `mycounter` to 655360, since there are 65536 scaled points to the point. Computer scientists call this process *coercion*, and you will see that a skip may be coerced to a length which may be coerced to a counter integer.

11.6   Boxes

A box is a register that can hold a piece of typeset text of arbitrary size. A single character is represented as an indivisible box in TEX. There are three kinds of boxes handled by LᴬTEX — *hboxes* which can contain a single line of text, *vboxes* (also known as *parboxes*) which can contain multiple lines broken up into paragraphs and *rules* which are rectangular blobs of ink. Once LᴬTEX has made a box, its contents are treated as an indivisible unit thereafter, so a common use of boxes is to inhibit line or page breaking. A *strut* is a special kind of rule that is zero points wide and therefore invisible. However, it still has height and can therefore be used as a fixed length spacer. The command \strut typesets a strut that is exactly the height of the current font. In maths mode, the equivalent command is \mathstrut. Struts are useful for placing rules correctly: for instance the commands $\overline{a}bc\underline{d}$ produce the rather disappointing $\overline{a}bc\underline{d}$, but by inserting struts thus

$\overline{\mathstrut a}bc\overline{\mathstrut d}$

we get the much more pleasing

$$\overline{a}bc\overline{d}$$

11.6.1 Hboxes

The LᴬTEX hbox commands come in long and abbreviated forms:

\mbox{*text*}
   puts *text* together into a box exactly wide enough to hold the characters. No line breaks can occur within the box, thus disabling hyphenation.

\makebox[*width*][*position*]{*text*}
   puts *text* into a box of predefined width. If the optional arguments are missing then \makebox is exactly the same as \mbox. If *width* is present, then it specifies the horizontal extent of the box, which may be greater or less than the space actually required for *text*. By default the text will be centred in the box, overhanging the sides if necessary. This can be overridden using the second optional argument. [l] left aligns the text ('flushleft') and [r] right aligns it ('flushright'). The flushing is done by automatically inserting a fill.

\fbox{*text*}
   exactly as for \mbox except that a frame is added around *text*.

\framebox[*width*][*position*]{*text*}
   exactly as for \makebox except that a frame is put around *text*.

11.6.2 Vboxes

In the LᴬTEX book vboxes are called parboxes. They are generated automatically as the output of the line breaking part of TEX, but you can make parboxes explicitly with the \parbox command, and this is often useful when you want to group a block of text together and then place it anywhere other than the left margin. The example letter shown in Figure 3.1 has the address set in a block and placed on the right hand margin. This is done inside the `letter` style by putting my address in a parbox, and then setting a fill and the parbox next to each other. The `\fill` spring right-justifies the box, pushing it over to the right margin.

Parboxes are often used as parameters to commands that can only cope with one dimensional lines of text, such as the text parameters to the picture mode `\framebox` command. These commands do not 'know' the width of the line at the time they are processed, so they can not cope with line break commands, because they would not know where to restart the line. The whole point of a parbox is that you *are* able to explicitly specify the linewidth to be used so that the line breaking algorithm can work.

There are two parbox making commands:

> `\parbox[`*position*`]{`*width*`}{`*text*`}`
>
> typesets *text* into paragraphs with each line being *width* long. Since the line breaking algorithm has to know in advance what the width of a paragraph is, the *width* argument is mandatory here unlike for hboxes. The optional *position* argument specifies the vertical alignment of the box with the text line. If *position* is absent then the centre of the box will line up with the text line. `[t]` forces the top of the box to align with the text line so that the box hangs down. `[b]` forces the bottom of the box up to the text line so that the box sits above the line.

> `\begin{minipage}[`*position*`]{`*width*`}` *text* `\end{minipage}`
>
> specifies that *text* be set in a `minipage` environment which is a sort of super parbox. It mimics the layout of a complete page with indented paragraphs, footnotes and so on. The large example in Chapter 1 was constructed using `minipage`. As you might expect `minipage` requires an explicit width and an optional positioning argument: the meanings of these arguments is the same as for the `\parbox` command.

11.6.3   Rules

Rules are made with `\rule[`*vshift*`]{`*width*`}{`*height*`}` which produces a black rectangle of size *width* $\times$ *height* sitting on the text baseline. The optional *vshift* argument (which may be positive or negative) specifies a vertical offset.

An interesting special case of a rule box is the `\strut`. A strut is a rule of zero width which is therefore invisible. There are places where a `\vspace` command does not work because LaTeX is in the middle of typesetting a paragraph, and in these cases a strut can be used to force the desired spacing.

11.6.4   Saveboxes

A box register is declared with `\newsavebox{`*boxname*`}` by analogy with `\newlength` and `\newcounter`. There are two commands to put things in a savebox:

`\sbox{`*boxname*`}{`*text*`}`

> typesets text as for an \mbox and places it in *boxname*. No text is
> output to the page.

`\savebox{`*boxname*`}[`*width*`] [`*position*`]{`*text*`}`

> typesets *text* exactly as for the corresponding \makebox command
> except that no output is produced, the result being placed in the
> box register instead.

A `\usebox{`*boxname*`}` command recalls the text. There can be many \usebox commands each typesetting a copy of the contents of *boxname*. Using saveboxes speeds TEX up at the cost of some internal memory (which is really quite limited, so don't get carried away). Probably the most appropriate use of saveboxes is in the picture environment, where complicated graphics objects may take a long time to process as illustrated in Figure 7.4.

11.6.5   Specifying exact box placement

A *raisebox* is the same kind of one-dimensional hbox as an mbox, but it can be moved above or below the line of text in which it sits. In addition, you can tell TEX that it is higher or lower than necessary just to contain the text, and this can be used to force vertical interline space.

`\raisebox{`*length*`}[`*above*`] [`*below*`]{`*text*`}`

> typesets *text* in an hbox and then displaces it vertically by *length*,
> which may be negative. A positive *length* raises the box and a neg-
> ative *length* lowers it. The optional *above* and *below* arguments
> are used to insert struts which make the box appear to extend
> above and below the text line by the specified amounts.

The glue and box commands described in this chapter can be used to construct almost any text placement, but they require you to think in a rather specialised way. If you really *must* have very exact spacing then try using the picture environment, which allows you to specify co-ordinates directly. It is worth remembering that an entire picture environment (and for that matter tabular and array environments too) generate a single box, which may be used as an overlarge character in normal typesetting. I once had to typeset some business cards, which required very careful alignment of the text in a complicated pattern. After wrestling with boxes and glue I admitted defeat and produced the right result using a picture environment with no fuss. This kind of thing makes plain TEX purists tear their hair out though, so keep quiet about it.

11.7   Parameter charts

The rest of this chapter lists the lengths and counters that you can manipulate directly. Most of the length parameters are illustrated using diagrams that show how LATEX builds pages.

11.8   Page style parameters

Figure 11.3 shows the details of page construction. You know by now that each page has a header, a footer, left and right margins and a text body. If you are using the [twocolumn] document option or the \twocolumn command then the body will be divided vertically into two equal halves. The text areas are shown here using dashed boxes and the page boundary is marked with a solid line. Perhaps surprisingly, the LaTeX origin is not the top left of the page, but a point 1 inch in from the corner vertically and horizontally.

When TeX builds a page it essentially works left to right and top to bottom. As a result, most of the offsets are only specified with respect to the left and top margins. There is no direct way of specifying the bottom of the page position for instance, it being simply the sum of all the vertical offsets. If TeX ends up building a page that is too big to be printed, then some of the text will simply be lost at the DVI driver stage[1]. TeX itself will not attempt to truncate the text.

\hoffset and \voffset move the entire TeX page with respect to the printed page. They can be negative, which allows you to have less than the 1 inch margins which TeX usually supplies.

Working inwards from left to right, the \oddsidemargin and \evensidemargin lengths specify the distance from the origin to the left edge of the text body. For double sided printing these will be different for the left and right (even and odd) pages, to allow for the binding. In single sided documents, all pages are right handed (odd), so the value of \evensidemargin is irrelevant.

Marginal note placement can be in either the left or right margins depending on the style file and whether any \reversemarginpar commands are in effect. In each case, the notes are formatted by typesetting them in parboxes that are \marginparwidth wide and them placing them \marginparsep away from the text body. As a result, altering \oddsidemargin or \evensidemargin shifts all the text, body and marginal notes together.

Marginal notes are usually vertically aligned with the point in the text body where they are defined. However, they must be vertically separated by at least \marginparpush, and they will be moved if necessary. A warning message is issued whenever a marginal note moves. In single column mode, the text body will be \textwidth wide and \textheight high. If two column typesetting is in force then the width of each column will one half of \textwidth−\columnsep , and they will be set \columnsep apart. A vertical rule of width \columnseprule will be typeset between them. By default, \columnseprule is 0pt so the rule is invisible. A width of 0.4pt will produce a rule of the width shown in the figure.

Working from top to bottom, the header and footer are typeset in hboxes of width \textwidth and of height \headheight and \footheight respectively. If you want multiline headers and footers, use a parbox of width \textwidth as a parameter to the \markboth or \markright commands.

The header will be separated by at least \headsep from the text body. The skips \topskip and \footskip are stretchable lengths.

---

[1]If you are unlucky, your DVI driver will get confused, but ideally it will just print the visible part of the text.

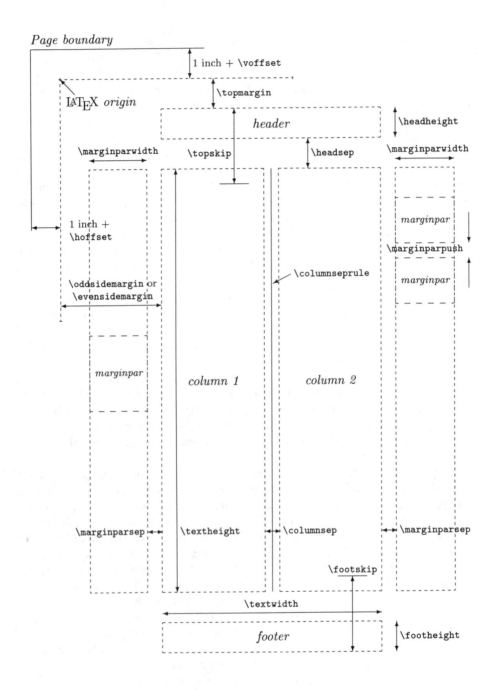

Figure 11.3 Page parameters

11.9   Paragraph parameters

Within a column, or the main text body in single column mode the spacings shown in Figure 11.9 are used. The paragraphs are \linewidth wide. At the outermost level in single column mode, \linewidth will be the same as \textwidth, but every environment such as quote that indents the margins will reduce \linewidth accordingly. The paragraphs are separated by \parskip. Since this is a skip (as opposed to a length) the paragraphs may be pulled apart as necessary to balance the page.

Within a paragraph, the baseline of each text line is separated vertically by \baselineskip from its neighbours. The first paragraph after a heading is never indented, but subsequent paragraphs will have a \parindent space inserted at the beginning. Many people express surprise that LaTeX does not indent the first paragraph in a section, but this is standard typesetting practice as you will see if you open any commercially typeset book[2].

\footnoterule is a command (not a length) that draws the footnote separator. You can use \renewcommand to define peculiar separators if you wish. When TeX builds the page, it assumes that the footnote separator defined by \footnoterule takes no vertical space, so you must compensate for the height of your separator by inserting a negative space of exactly the right height to ensure that the footers for pages with footnotes match the footer separation of normal pages. The footnotes themselves are typeset in parboxes the same width as the text column separated by skips of height \footnotesep. The running footnote number is maintained in the counter footnote. As you might expect, the printed footnote number is produced with \thefootnote, which you can redefine to get unusual numbering conventions. Within a minipage environment, the counter mpfootnote and the command \thempfootnote are used instead, so as to avoid disrupting the main run of footnotes.

11.10   List style parameters

The list environment is LaTeX's central mechanism for producing indented structures and is used to define quote and quotation as well as the more obvious itemize and enumerate:

```
\begin{list}{default-label}{declarations}
\item first body
\item second body
   ⋮
\end{list}
```

default-label is used to form the item labels in the absence of an optional parameter to the \item command. The commands in declarations are executed

---

[2]I once had to prove this to my students by getting them to pick a book at random from my shelves and check for themselves. They went away satisfied, and I did not bother to point out that the book they had chosen had been typeset in LaTeX... Nevertheless, it is still true.

3.5 A section heading

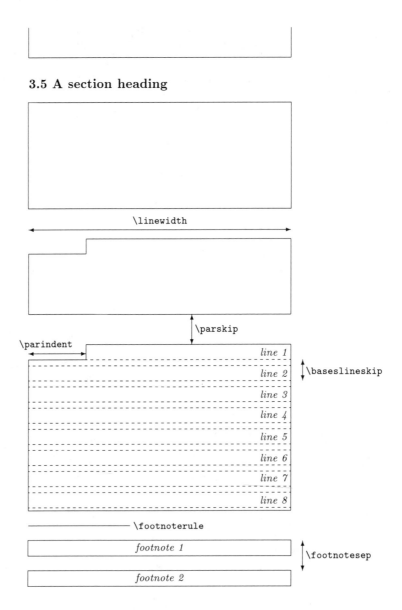

Figure 11.4 Paragraph parameters

at the start of the environment to set up the indentation and font style. Before calling *declarations*, LaTeX executes the command \@list$n$ where n is i, ii, iii or iv increasing with list nesting. Roman numerals are used because arabic digits may not appear in TeX control words. The \@list$n$ commands are defined in the style file.

The layout of a general list is shown in Figure 11.5. A list comprises a sequence of labelled *items* each of which may have a multiparagraph body. The labels and the bodies are indented, and normal paragraph indentation works within a body, that is the first paragraph is not indented but subsequent ones are. Lists may be nested to a maximum depth of five.

The indentation of the item bodies is specified by the parameters \leftmargin and \rightmargin. In an itemize environment, labels are constructed by executing the command \labelitem$n$ where n is a roman number in the range i to iv. At the outermost level, \labelitemi is used, at the first nested level \labelitemii is used and so on. In other environments you can override the default label by redefining the command \makelabel{*labeltext*} which is called by LaTeX to typeset the labels.

The label will be typeset right flushed in an hbox of width \labelwidth. If the label is wider then \labelwidth then the box will expand to exactly fit it. The left hand edge of the label will always be at a point

$$\text{\textbackslash leftmargin} - \text{\textbackslash labelwidth} - \text{\textbackslash labelsep} + \text{\textbackslash itemindent}$$

in from the left hand margin of the enclosing text. Normally \itemindent is 0pt, giving the kind of spacing shown for the first and second items in Figure 11.5. However, if you do set \itemindent to a positive value, the label will shift right, and the first line of the body will be indented to ensure that there is still \labelsep worth of space between the label and the start of the text. Subsequent lines will be indented as for a normal body. This effect is shown in the third item of the figure.

The fourth item in the figure shows that a similar indentation occurs if the label is wider than \labelwidth: the \labelsep wide gap between the label and the body will be maintained by indenting the first paragraph of the body.

The entire list will be separated by \topsep + \parskip worth of whitespace from the preceding and following text. An extra space of \partopsep will be inserted if the list begins a paragraph, i.e. if it is preceded by a blank line or a \par command. A gap of \itemsep + \parsep will be inserted between each item body, and within an item body the paragraphs are separated by \parsep and indented by \listparindent.

The details of the default parameters for each environment are set by the style file. Some of the parameters are initialised within the \begin{*environment name*} command, so you will need to adjust them *within* the environment.

A rather specialised list, the bibliography environment, uses the parameter \bibindent to specify the indentation of long bibliography items when the openbib style option is in use.

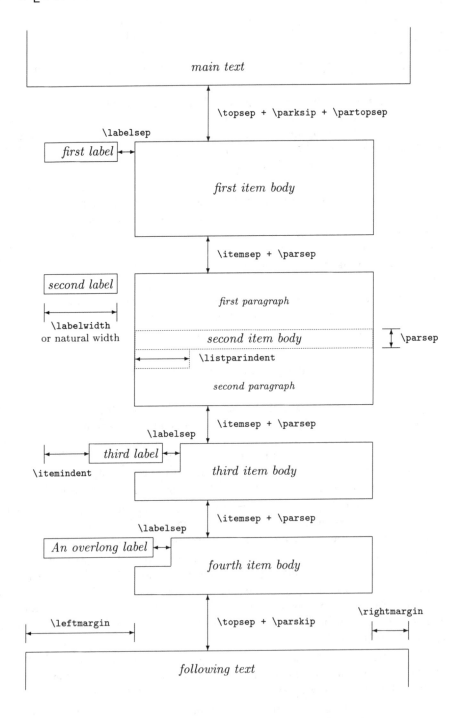

Figure 11.5 List parameters

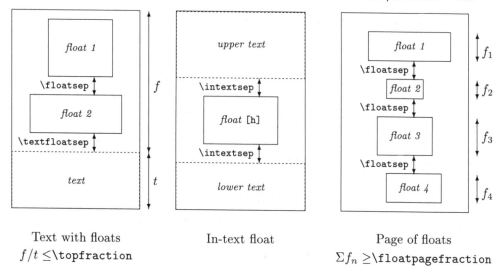

Figure 11.6 Float parameters

11.11   Float parameters

Floats can appear in three different contexts: the in-text float made with an [h] option, a page of floats forced with a [p] option or created automatically if there is sufficient pending float material to fill a page, and the usual text-with-floats page where the floats live at the top or bottom depending on whether a [t] or [b] option was used. These three cases are illustrated in Figure 11.6.

Float placement can be a source of some dissatisfaction amongst LaTeX users. The [h] optional argument to the `table` and `figure` environments *should* create an in-text float, i.e. a non-floating float. In practice, LaTeX is quite fussy and will in fact move a float unless there is plenty of space on the page.

11.11.1   Vertical float spacing

In-text floats are separated from the surrounding text by \intextsep, and you might try reducing this to zero if you absolutely *must* force a float to appear inline.

Where a sequence of floats is output, either on a page of floats or on text with floats page, a skip of \floatsep will be inserted between the floats. Since this space is a skip, the gap may be stretched as necessary. Except for in-text floats, a skip of \textfloatsep will be inserted between floats and adjacent text.

11.11.2   Limiting the number of floats on a page

A page of floats is allowed when there are enough floats in the queue to fill at least \floatpagefraction of a page. Perhaps surprisingly, \floatpagefraction is a command, so it is redefined using a command of the form

```
\renewcommand{\floatpagefraction}{.75}
```

The reason this parameter is a command and not a counter is that L<small>A</small>T_EX counters can only hold integers, not fractions.

For a mixed text and float page, the counters `topnumber` and `bottomnumber` specify the maximum number of floats that may appear at the top and bottom of the page respectively. The counter `totalnumber` limits the total number of floats that may appear on a page under any circumstances. A mixed page must have at least `\textfraction` occupied by text. Like `\floatpagefraction` it is a command, and must be redefined using `\renewcommand`.

11.11.3   Double page parameters

When two column formatting is in force (either after a `\twocolumn` command or when the `[twocolumn]` style option is used) an alternate set of parameters is used. The five parameters `\dbltopfraction`, `\dblfloatpagefraction`, `dbltopnumber`, `\dblfloatsep` and `\dbltextfloatsep` perform the same functions for two column text as the parameters `\topfraction`, `\floatpagefraction` and so on do for single column printing.

11.12   Display maths parameters

Maths displays are created using the `displaymath` environment or the `\[ ...\]` commands. Formulae in display maths environments are classified as either *short* or *long* depending on whether they start to the right of the end of the last line or not. Short formulae have `\aboveshortdisplayskip` inserted before them and `\belowshortdisplayskip` above. Long formulae have `\abovedisplayskip` inserted before them and `\belowdisplayskip` below.

In the `fleqn` document option, `\topsep` is used for all inter-formulae spaces, and `\mathindent` is use to indent formulae from the left margin.

11.13   Tabular and array parameters

The `tabular` environment and its maths-mode equivalent `array` are useful for general typesetting as well as for tables because the output is a single box. Rather complex superscripts may be built up for instance by using an `array` environment to arrange items in a grid and then supply the entire environment as an argument to the `^` command. The parameters shown in Figure 11.7 must be changed *within* the environment because they are reinitialised by the `\begin{tabular}` and `\begin{array}` commands.

The default inter-row spacing may be stretched by redefining the command `\arraystretch`. Its default value is 1, and increasing it moves rows apart whilst decreasing it pushes them together. When multiple adjacent vertical or horizontal lines are typeset they will be separated by `\doublerulesep`. Note that vertical lines are broken across double horizontal lines since the vertical line only fills the text part of a row. The actual width of horizontal and vertical lines is specified

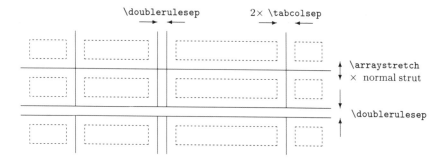

Figure 11.7 Tabular and array parameters

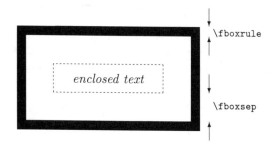

Figure 11.8 Frame parameters

by \arrayrulewidth. A value of 0.4pt will give lines like those in the figure. A space of \tabcolsep (or \arraycolsep in an array environment) is appended and prepended to all items in a row, so the default spacing is $2 \times$ \tabcolsep will be used between columns. This spacing is suppressed for columns with an @-expression in their specification. In an eqnarray environment, extra vertical space specified by the command \jot is added between rows.

11.14   Framebox parameters

The text in a framebox is set in an hbox exactly large enough to fit round the text. A whitespace border of width \fboxsep is then placed around the box, and then rules of width \fboxrule are drawn all the way round. These parameters are shown in Figure 11.8.

11.15   Sectioning parameters

Each sectioning command has an associated depth, as listed in section 4.3. For every sectioning command there is an associated counter of the same name and a command to print it. So for the \subsection command, the present subsection number is held in the subsection counter and the definition of \thesubsection specifies the way it will be printed. Each counter is zeroed when its enclosing section number is incremented. The sectioning commands below the level of \chapter will print the section numbers down to the depth specified in the counter secnumdepth. A good value for this parameter is 2, which will print headings of the form

chapter.section.subsection

but leave the number off for subsubsections and below.

Table of contents generation is controlled using the counter tocdepth which specifies the maximum depth of section heading that will be listed in the table of contents. Again, 2 is a good value to use.

11.16   Default parameter values

The large number of parameters listed in this chapter are all initialised in the style file. The next chapter explains the contents of the standard style files, and shows you where to find the initialisation code for the style parameters.

12

Writing a style file

This chapter is about the internal workings of LaTeX. TeX itself is a complex and subtle system, and the combined LaTeX source code runs to some 11,000 lines, so a single chapter is in no sense going to offer a complete guide to LaTeX programming. Instead, I shall concentrate on the structure of the standard style files and explain enough about TeX's commands to enable you to make simple modifications to the existing styles. If you want to really get to grips with TeX programming, then you should consider a copy of the TeXbook [Knu86a] a mandatory purchase. I have also found *A Beginner's Book of TeX* by Raymond Seroul and Silvio Levy a useful reference [SL91]. You may be able to get a copy of the document *A Gentle Introduction to TeX* by Michael Doob [Doo] from your supplier or system manager — this is a freely available booklet that has been translated into several European languages. Finally, *TeX for the Beginner* by Wynter Snow [Sno92] is particularly suitable for LaTeX users since it describes plain TeX but cross references to LaTeX features.

12.1 The LaTeX format

Although LaTeX is so large, it is all written in the TeX language which is readable by humans (with some patience and training). The source code is always distributed with a LaTeX system, and it is heavily commented so in principle every aspect of the system's implementation can be understood by the persistent user.

It would be very inefficient for TeX to read in and process all 11,000 lines of the LaTeX macro package every time you started to process a document, so TeX has a mechanism for reading pre-digested macros from a *format file*. A special version of TeX called IniTeX is used to create these format files[1]. The LaTeX format is constructed from four files — lplain.tex, latex.tex, lfonts.tex and hyphen.tex. lplain is the master file, so a new format file may be created by changing directory to your inputs directory[2] and then typing something like

    initex lplain

At the end of rather a lot of processing, TeX will stop and issue a * prompt. You should respond with \dump which is a special IniTeX command that causes the

---

[1]Sometimes there is no separate initex program, but the normal TeX program is used with a special switch. See Appendix A.

[2]See page 24.

format file to be written out, and control to be returned to the operating system. You should move the new format file to the place on your system where format files are kept. This location is rather system specific, so consult the documentation for your version of TEX. Normally you will never need to rebuild the LATEX format.

lplain.tex is a slightly modified version of plain.tex, the standard format that Knuth wrote for everyday TEX use. Some commands are commented out, and there are enough differences between lplain and plain to ensure that only very simple plain documents will pass through LATEX unscathed. lplain reads in and processes hyphen.tex, another file from the original TEX system that defines American hyphenation patterns. In principle, you can replace hyphen.tex with a file specific to your own language, but the construction of a new set of hyphenation patterns is a non-trivial task. It is especially important for foreign languages, because TEX will not usually hyphenate a word that contains an accent command. New patterns are available for German and some other European languages.

After processing the hyphenation patterns lplain goes on to read in lfonts.tex in which all of the font changing commands such as \bf are associated with particular TEX fonts such as cmbx. If you look in lfonts.tex you will find that other font styles such as \sfb (the **bold sans-serif** font used for section headings in this book) and \tti (an *italic teletype* font) are defined, but commented out, as many versions of TEX do not have enough internal memory to hold all of the necessary definitions. If you want to use these fonts and you have a big TEX implementation you could uncomment the definitions and rebuild the LATEX format. However, this is a bad idea for two reasons — firstly you will have a non-standard version of LATEX and so you might have difficulties exchanging documents with other users, but more importantly because there is a completely new font selection scheme available that offers much greater flexibility. You will find details of the new font selection scheme (NFSS) and how to obtain it in the next chapter.

Right at the end, lplain calls in latex.tex, a large file which contains the vast bulk of the LATEX system. This is the file you should read if you want to know how a particular command is implemented.

12.2 How style files fit in

Some parts of LATEX are not fully defined in the main latex.tex file. These parts include the full specification of the \section command and the details of float processing. Every document must read in a file that completes these definitions before processing begins, and that file is usually the *primary style file*, defined in a \documentstyle like:

```
\documentstyle[11pt,bezier]{article}
```

LATEX expects a \documentstyle command to be the first thing in your file (apart from comments and blank lines) and it processes it by, in this case, looking for and processing a file called article.sty in the inputs directory. The optional argument contains a comma separated list of items which may be the names of additional files, or may be commands directly understood by the primary style file article. In this case, 11pt is a command to the style file that indirectly causes it to read in the file art11.sty which defines fonts for the 11pt version of `article`, and `bezier` is the name of the file that defines the `\bezier` command described in section 7.5.8.

Files like `bezier.sty` are not dependant on any particular primary style and really exist to add extra specialist commands to LaTeX. Files like `art11.sty` are an integral part of the `article` style, and are not useful on their own.

It is important to find out what styles are available to you, which you can do by checking the inputs directory of your computer for filenames ending in `.sty`. Style files are written in the TeX language, and there may be comments in the `.sty` file that explain the functionality of the style. If there are none, try looking for a file with the same name but a `.doc` filetype, which will be a more human friendly version of the style.

12.3   Internal and external commands

If you look in a style file or in the LaTeX source files you will see a large number of @ signs. There is a convention that command words which are internal (or *local*) to a style have an @ sign in the name, whereas command words that are available for use in the document have only letters in their name. In fact TeX provides a way of enforcing this convention, and it will normally refuse to even recognise a command name with an @ in it in your document. This is to make sure that you do not accidentally define a command that might conflict with one of LaTeX's internal names, or accidentally misuse an internal command.

You can override this behaviour with the command `\makeatletter` which makes the @ sign behave like a letter so that TeX will recognise it as a valid constituent of a command name. The command `\makeatother` returns @ to its non-letter state, restoring the default LaTeX behaviour. You may occasionally find it useful to access internal commands, but be sure to only switch the behaviour of the @ sign when you need to as very peculiar errors can occur if you unintentionally use an internal command.

Within style files, `\makeatletter` is automatically in force. `\makeatother` is executed immediately after processing the last style file before handing control back to your document file.

12.4   The rudiments of TeX programming

The TeX language was designed to be compact and easy to write as opposed to easy to read. Most computer languages have a clearly visible structure featuring keywords which have a fixed meaning, and this is a great help when trying to read someone else's code, as the keywords provide a 'skeleton' into which the program's actions fit. TeX, however, is a *macro expansion language* with very few keywords and a large number of primitive commands that are not obviously distinguished from user definitions, so the process of understanding a TeX program may involve unravelling many layers of macro expansion to arrive at a long sequence of primitive commands.

To add to the confusion, almost nothing in TeX need be what it seems. Even the \ escape character can be changed (although it almost never is in LaTeX), and in some contexts characters have different meanings. A trivial example of this is the \verb command which turns off all TeX character interpretation between two delimiter characters.

Fortunately, the kind of TeX programming found inside style files is usually straightforward, and you will not run up against any real TeX trickery unless you start reading `latex.tex`. This section explains the TeX commands that are used in the standard styles, but should not be interpreted as a complete guide to TeX programming.

12.4.1   TeX definitions

A TeX definition creates a new command. The LaTeX commands \newcommand and \renewcommand also perform this function, but they are rather inefficient because they go to some lengths to catch errors. In addition, there are some circumstances that require special features not provided to the LaTeX user. As a result the style files almost always use the underlying TeX definition commands.

12.4.2   \def and its variants

The command

\def*command*{*text*}

associates *text* with *command* as would a \newcommand{*command*}{*text*} command. No check is made to see whether *command* is already defined. The *text* parameter must not contain a blank line or a \par command—that is the expansion must not include the end of a paragraph. This rule catches the common error of forgetting to append the closing brace to the {*text*} argument. When TeX sees the end of a paragraph inside a definition it issues a **Runaway argument?** error message.

In some circumstances it is necessary to define an expansion *text* which is more than one paragraph long. In such cases, the \def command is prepended by \long, so

\long\def*command*{*text with paragraph breaks*}

can have arbitrary text in the expansion argument, but of course TeX will not be able to catch any missing } errors.

There is another \def modifier that is used to restrict the context in which the defined command may be used. If you precede the \def with \outer then the new command will only be recognised by TeX when it is at its 'outermost' level of processing. In particular, the macro will not be accepted in the arguments to any other commands.

There are a few LaTeX definitions that are *global*, that is they are remembered throughout a document, as opposed to normal definitions which are forgotten at the end of their enclosing group. You can create a global definition by prefacing the \def command with \global. For those that do not like typing, there is also a TeX primitive \gdef which is equivalent to \global\def.

The modifiers \long, \outer and \global can appear in any order and in any combination before the \def command.

12.4.3   Definitions with parameters

The LaTeX \newcommand and \renewcommand sequences allow commands with parameters to be defined by supplying an optional argument containing the number of parameters to be used. The TEX \def command can have up to nine parameters numbered #1 – #9. A command of the form

```
\def\mycommand#1#2#3{$#1=#3^#2$}
```

will typeset expressions of the form $x = z^y$ when called with \mycommand{x}{y}{z}. You must request parameters in order: \def\mycommand#1#4 is an error because parameters 2 and 3 must be used before parameter 4. However, parameters can appear in the replacement text in any order and as many times as you like.

A particularly tricky aspect of TEX's parameter definitions is the use of *delimited* parameters. It is most important to ensure that there are no intervening characters between the parameters in the definition, because if there are TEX will take them as boundary characters for the macro expansion. These commands

```
\def\funnycommand#1=#2.#3..{Whole part #2, fractional part #3}
\funnycommand x=16.385..
```

produce

Whole part 16, fractional part 385

When TEX sees any characters appearing in the parameter list for a \def it remembers them and uses them to divide up the text following a call to that macro. In this case, TEX will take everything after the \funnycommand up to the first = sign as the first parameter, everything from there to the first . as the second and everything up to a pair of . characters as the third. This powerful feature allows TEX parameters to be almost any piece of text, but can wreak havoc if you accidentally leave some blanks between the #n parameter definitions. LaTeX eschews such cleverness and insists that all parameters are simply delimited by {} braces, which makes LaTeX code easier to read if less flexible.

12.4.4   Command assignments

The command \let\newcommand=\oldcommand gives \newcommand the same definition as \oldcommand. This more efficient than \def\newcommand{\oldcommand} because it saves one level of macro expansion in the interpretation of \newcommand.

\newcommand is *not* always a synonym for \oldcommand because after a \let command you can change the definition of \oldcommand but \newcommand will retain the previous definition.

12.4.5 Grouping

The usual way of making a group in TEX is with the {} braces. There are a pair of commands \begingroup and \endgroup that have the same effect as { and } but braces must be matched with braces, and \begingroup must be matched with \endgroup. These two variants are an aid in error checking — LATEX environments use the \begingroup ... \endgroup pair and can therefore catch any unmatched braces inside them.

There is a subtle problem with the definition of macros that are to be used to sandwich other blocks of text. A macro definition may not contain unmatched braces, because braces are also used to delimit the macro replacement text. The only way to get unmatched braces into a macro definition is to use the special commands \bgroup and \egroup which are alternative names for { and } (created with \let commands) that may be used in macro definitions without TEX 'noticing' that they are really braces.

12.4.6 TEX control flow

Any programming language needs statements to change the flow of a control. TEX has a mechanism for defining and using conditionals, and allows macros to call themselves which enables code to be repeatedly executed.

12.4.7 TEX conditionals

A conditional statement has the following form

>   \if*condition* *true-text* \else *false-text* \fi

When TEX comes across a conditional, it evaluates *condition* and if it is true the entire statement including the \if and the \fi is deleted and replaced with *true-text*. If the *condition* is false then the statement is replaced with *false-text*. It is important to realise that the conditional simply chooses between two replacement texts: it does not in any sense execute either branch, and it does not matter if the *true-text* or *false-text* are in themselves correct TEX sequences as long as after replacement a well-formed TEX sequence results. In particular, the *true-* and *false-text* can contain unbalanced braces. If the *false-text* is null, then the entire \else *false-text* clause may be omitted.

A large number of different *condition*s are predefined. Some of them depend on TEX features that we have not described so only a selection are listed here.

>   \ifodd*number* *true-text* \else *false-text* \fi
>   tests whether a literal number, a count register, a length interpreted
>   as scaled points or the natural length of a skip interpreted as scaled
>   points is odd.

>   \ifnum *number* *rel* *number* *true-text* \else *false-text* \fi
>   tests a relation between two numbers, which may be any mix of lit-
>   eral numbers, count registers, lengths interpreted as scaled points,
>   or the natural length of a skip interpreted as scaled points.

rel may be <, = or >=.

`\ifdim` *number rel number true-text* `\else` *false-text* `\fi`
  tests a relation between two dimensions, which may be any mix of
  literal lengths, length registers or the natural length of a skip.
  rel may be <, = or >=.

`\ifcasenumber text0` `\or` *text1* `\or` ... `\else` *else-text* `\fi`
  Perform a multiway branch (a *case* statement) by looking at the
  value of *number* and replacing the entire conditional statement with
  the nth branch, *textn*. If the number is negative, or if it is greater
  than the number of `\or` clauses then replace the conditional with
  the *else-text*.

12.4.8   User defined conditionals

A common requirement is to have a *switch* which controls formatting. An example
from LaTeX is the switch that controls whether two-column printing is in force.
The `\twocolumn` command and the `{twocolumn}` style option must set this switch,
and the `\onecolumn` command must reset it. One way to implement this might
be to reserve a counter register, assign an odd or even number to it and test it
with an `\ifnum` command. This is rather wasteful of resources, since an entire
numeric register is being used to hold a quantity which can have only two states (a
Boolean variable in computer science-speak) so TeX allows you to define your own
conditionals.

The command `\newif\if`*myswitch* defines three new control sequences

`\`*myswitch*`true`
  which sets *myswitch* true

`\`*myswitch*`false`
  which sets *myswitch* false

`\if`*myswitch* *true-text* `\else` *false-text* `\fi`
  which tests the value of *myswitch* and replaces the entire conditional statement with *true-text* or *false-text* accordingly.

12.4.9   TeX loops

TeX allows macro replacement texts to contain calls to themselves, which means
that a macro can be repeatedly evaluated. This self-reference is called *recursion*,
and it is an unfortunate fact of life that non-mathematicians seem to find recursion
difficult to understand, which is a great shame. The plain TeX format defines a
command that performs iteration in a more comprehensible fashion:

`\loop` *pre-test-text* `\if`*condition* *post-test-text* `\repeat`

TeX will process *pre-test-text* and then evaluate the *condition*. If it is true,
then *post-test-text* will be processed and the whole loop will be repeated. If the
condition is false then processing will continue with the text after the `\repeat`

command. Note that the \if clause is *not* a fully formed conditional statement, but just the \if*condition* part with no replacement texts or matching \fi command.

This command is retained in lplain.tex, and may be used in style files and documents. LaTeX also has some iteration and conditional commands of its own that are described in the next section.

12.4.10   The LaTeX ifthen style commands

If you include the [ifthen] document style option then the following two commands will be defined:

\ifthenelse{*test*}{*true-text*}{*false-text*}
> evaluate *test* and replace the entire command with either *true-text* or *false-text* accordingly.

\whiledo{*test*}{*while-text*}
> evaluate *test* and if it is true execute the *while-text* and restart at the \whiledo command, otherwise continue with the command after the \whiledo.

The *test* argument in these commands allows natural logical phrases to be constructed. The basic tests are

\equal{*text1*}{*text2*} All of the macros in *text1* and *text2* are expanded and then the test returns true if the results are identical.

number rel number where *rel* may be < = or >

These simple tests may be combined into Boolean expressions using the commands \and, \or, \not and brackets \(and \).

These LaTeX constructions are far closer to the control statements found in conventional procedural programming languages like C and Pascal than TeX's macro-like conditionals.

12.4.11   TeX modes

At the lowest level, TeX is a program for putting boxes together. At certain times TeX will refuse to execute some commands. For instance the LaTeX \\ end of line command can only be used when a line has actually been built up, otherwise you get the message There is no line to end here. TeX has six modes which govern what actions are allowable at a particular point in the text. The modes are closely related to the kinds of boxes that are being constructed, and you might find it helpful to review the material in section 11.6 before reading further.

When TeX is building paragraphs, it first gathers all the characters together in a long one-dimensional line. At this time TeX is in *horizontal mode*. If you are collecting characters to go into an hbox, which will never be split up into lines (for instance whilst processing the argument to an \mbox command) then TeX is in *restricted horizontal mode*.

After a whole paragraph has been found, the long line built in horizontal mode is divided up into lines of about the right width to fit on the page. TeX enters *vertical* mode and attempts to fit these boxes onto the page looking for good page breaks. When TeX is making a vbox, as is the case during the construction of a float or a `tabular` environment, it continues to pile up lines and will not look for page breaks. This mode is called *restricted vertical mode*. It is restricted in the same sense as restricted horizontal mode: restricted vertical mode ignores potential page breaks and continues vertically; restricted horizontal mode ignore potential line breaks and continues horizontally.

The last two TeX modes are both used for typesetting mathematics. *Maths mode* is used to typeset in-line formulae found between $ \ldots $ signs, and *display maths mode* is used for `equation` environments and display maths formulae found between \[\ldots \] commands.

By and large you will not need to keep track of these modes when using LaTeX, but it is sometimes necessary to engineer a mode change within a style file. The command \par denotes the end of a paragraph (as does a blank line) and forces TeX into vertical mode, as does any vertical spacing command. TeX returns to horizontal mode whenever a character is typeset or when horizontal spacing commands are encountered. Restricted horizontal mode is entered by using commands like \mbox or \makebox, and restricted vertical mode is entered within floats, `tabular` and `array` environments, and the `picture` environment.

12.4.12   Penalties

When TeX is looking for good line or page breaks it performs calculations that compute the *badness* of the break. Having to hyphenate a word increases the badness of the break, as does an excess of whitespace on a line. If life were simple it would be possible to define absolute rules that would yield pleasingly balanced pages in all cases. In reality, it is sometimes necessary to tweak the probability of a line break occurring at a particular point. The command \penalty*number* inserts a *penalty* which is a hint to the breaking algorithms this is a good or bad place to make a break. A negative penalty *number* encourages a page or line break, and a positive penalty discourages. TeX actually squares the penalty value before feeding it into the breaking algorithms, so a penalty of 10 is much stronger than a penalty of 2. The maximum value of a penalty is 10000 and the minimum value -10000. A penalty of 0 does not affect the balance of the calculations, but it does allow line breaking at a point where it would not otherwise occur which is especially useful in long maths formulae.

The LaTeX styles define a series of commands that are synonyms for standard penalties, and there are some TeX primitive parameters that are used as penalty values, such as \hyphenpenalty which is the penalty added in to a tentative line break at a hyphenation point.

12.5   An overview of `article.sty`

The best way to learn to write a new style file is to learn how the standard styles work. The three main standard styles (`article`, `report` and `book`) are internally very similar. This section looks at each part of `article.doc`, the documentation file for the `article` style. You will find it useful to have a printout of `article.doc` available as you read this section.

12.5.1   Initialisation and internal options

There is an internal LaTeX command called `\@options` which is usually called near the beginning of the style file. This command causes LaTeX to process style options by looking at each part of the comma delimited list in the optional parameter to `\documentstyle` (if present) and for each one attempting to execute a command of the form `\ds@`*option* where *option* is the name of the option. For example, a command of the form

```
\documentstyle[twoside]{article}
```

calls up the `article` style and begins to process its contents.

When an `\@option` command is found LaTeX will attempt to execute the internal command `\ds@twoside`. Near the beginning of the `article` style file this command is defined as

```
\def\ds@twoside{\@twosidetrue \@mparswitchtrue}
```

Executing this command sets two conditions which tell LaTeX to use doublesided printing (i.e. use both the `\oddsidemargin` and the `\evensidemargin` page parameters) and put marginal notes in the outside margin.

In my version of `article.sty` a [draft] option is defined with

```
\def\ds@draft{\overfullrule 5pt}
```

`\overfullrule` is a TeX primitive that draws a black rule box at the end of any overfull hboxes. If you use the style option [draft] then LaTeX will place a 5pt wide rule at the end of any overfull line, which makes them very easy to spot on a draft print out. It is easy to redefine `\ds@draft` to insert the word DRAFT in the header or footer to ensure that a preliminary copy of your document does not accidentally get released to a wider audience.

12.5.2   Undefined options

If you request an option for which no corresponding `\ds@`*option* command exists in the primary style file, LaTeX will search the inputs directory for a file of the name *option*`.sty` and process that before continuing. If no such file exists, an error message will be issued. Usually, TeX searches the directory in which it was started before the inputs directory, so you can keep local copies of style files that will take precedence over the system defaults.

12.5.3   Type size suboption processing

The font size options are treated specially because they contain numeric digits. Normally, TeX refuses to recognise non-alphabetic characters in command names, but the document options mechanism requires us to define a command name `\ds@11pt` to handle the [11pt] option. It turns out that it is possible to persuade TEX to accept these unusual command names, and there is an internal LATEX command \@namedef which allows commands with any characters in the name to be defined. It is used the same way as \newcommand except that a leading \ is automatically supplied for the command name, so

```
\def\@ptsize{0}                        %initialise to 10pt
\@namedef{ds@11pt}{\def\@ptsize{1}}    %change to 11pt
\@namedef{ds@12pt}{\def\@ptsize{2}}    %change to 12pt

\input art1\@ptsize.sty
```

defines a command \@ptsize which will be used to supply the last digit of the file-name for the font size subsidiary style file. By default, its value is 0, but a document style option of [11pt] causes the command \ds@11pt to be executed which resets it to 1. Subsequently the \input command reads in the file art1*ds@11pt*.sty, i.e. art11.sty. Of course, the \@options command must come before the \input command to ensure that all options have been processed before the font file is read.

12.5.4   The typesize file

The three font size subsidiary style files all have the same form. The bulk of their content is a series of dimension, skip, penalty and font definitions that specify the size of a page, the base fonts to use and the line and page breaking behaviour. A great deal of work has gone into the specification of these parameters, and it would be wise to leave them alone unless you are a competent book designer. Most of the file should be easily modifiable if you have understood the discussion of LATEX lengths, counters and skips in the previous chapter.

Somewhat anomolously, all of the section commands used in `article` are defined in the font size file. This is because the typeset headings must be declared when the sectioning commands are created, and the spacings surrounding a section heading must vary with the size of the font. The definition of sectioning commands will be discussed in section 12.5.7 below.

12.5.5   Environments

When LATEX encounters a \begin{*environment*} command it starts a new group which declares a new scope level, performs some housekeeping and then attempts to execute the command *environment*. If this command is undefined then LATEX issues an Undefined environment error message. When LATEX reaches the corresponding \end{*environment*} it executes the \end*environment* command.

Some environments like itemize are an integral part of the LATEX source code, and some, such as quote are only defined in the style file so they do not appear in latex.tex. Many environments, including quote, quotation, verse and description are defined in terms of the primitive list environment described in section 11.10. In general, environments that are defined only in the style will have definitions for \environment and \endenvironment in the style file, whereas environments that are built into LaTeX will just have some parameters defined.

When the \begin command is processed, the internal command \@currenvir is set to the environment name. This is checked by the \end command to make sure that environment names are nested correctly. \@currenvir is initialised to document to make sure that the document is terminated with an \end{document} command.

LaTeX users are often a little vague in the spacing of their source files. There is a global conditional switch called @ignore which may be set using the command \global\@ignoretrue that causes LaTeX to throw blanks away, and it is sometimes useful to include this call in the definition of your \endenvironment command to consume any trailing whitespace after the corresponding \endenvironment command.

12.5.6 Enumerate and itemize

These environments are defined in latex.tex, but there are sets of commands and counters defined that may be manipulated in the style file to change the printed results. article supports up to four nested levels of enumerate and itemize.

Each level of enumeration has an associated counter enumi – enumiv. As is usual with counters there are commands \theenumi – \theenumiv that are used to print the counters out. In article, these commands use \arabic, \alph, \roman and \Alph for increasing levels of nesting.

The label in an enumerate environment is actually produced with the commands \labelenumi – \labelenumiv. The style file commands

```
\def\labelenumii{(\theenumii)}
\def\theenumii{\alph{enumii}}
```

produce labels of the form (c). These commands may be redefined in the style file or indeed in the document, because they do not have @ signs in their names.

The itemize environment is more straightforward because there are no counters to maintain. The style file defines four commands \labelitemi – \labelitemiv which are used to typeset the labels. By default, \labelitemi is defined to be $\bullet$.

12.5.7 Sectioning

The definition of the sectioning commands is split between the main style file and the font size subsidiary file. Section commands usually call the internal LaTeX command

```
\@startsection{name}{level}{indentation}
{aboveskip}{belowskip}{commands}
```

which performs the following actions in order:

1. Insert a vertical skip of size *aboveskip*.

2. Indent from the left margin by *indentation*.

3. Execute *commands* which typically set the font size and style for the section title.

4. If the `\name` command is *not* followed by a `*` and *level* is $\le$ the parameter `secnumdepth` then print the section number using the command `\thename` which must be defined in the style file. If a number is printed, increment the counter *name* which must be defined in the style file.

5. Insert a vertical skip of size *belowskip*.

So, in general each section must be defined with

◇ a call to `\@startsection`,

◇ a counter,

◇ a counter printing command.

In `article` the counter definitions are in `article.sty` and the actual sectioning commands are defined in `art1n.sty`. A typical set of definitions is

```
\def\subsection{\@startsection{subsection}{2}{\z@}{-3.25ex plus
-1ex minus .2ex}{1.5ex plus .2ex}{\normalsize\bf}

\newcounter{subsection}[section]
\def\thesubsection{\thesection.\arabic{subsection}}
```

The command `\z@` used in the indentation parameter is actually an abbreviation for 0pt. It saves space in TeX's internal memory because only one token is needed. Note that the `subsection` counter is enclosed by the `section` counter.

Also lurking in the subsidiary font style file is the definition of the `\appendix` command. This simply resets the `section` and `subsection` counters and redefines section number printing to use the `\Alph` style. The `secnumdepth` counter is also initialised here to 3.

12.5.8   Table of contents, list of figures and list of tables

When table of contents generation is in effect the sectioning commands write a file called *name*`.toc`. Each sectioning command outputs a line of the form

```
\contentsline{sectionname}{title}{pagenumber}
```

If the section is numbered (i.e. it was not a `*` form of the sectioning command and the `secnumdepth` counter did not suppress the section number) then *title* is written as `\numberline{section number}{heading}`, otherwise *title* will just be the printed section heading. The `\addcontentsline` command may be used to write lines of this format to the `.toc` file. The `\listoffigures` and `\listoftables` commands enable similar mechanisms that produce `.lof` and `.lot` files which have the same internal structure.

On the next LaTeX pass, these files are read back in, and each

```
\contentsline{sectionname}
```

is expanded to a command of the form `\@sectionname{title}{pagenumber}`. The format of contents pages is therefore specified simply by defining `\l@section`, `\l@subsection`, `\l@figure` and so on.

In `article` a contents entry comprises the *title* left justified (possibly with an indentation), a dotted line across the page (called a *leader* by printers) and *pagenumber*, right justified. The internal command

```
\@dottedtocline{level}{indent}{numwidth}{title}{pagenumber}
```

is used to generate the standard contents entries.

level is used to suppress the entry if its value is $\leq$ the `tocdepth` counter. *indent* is the indentation for this contents item, *numwidth* is the width of the box to contain the section number and *title* and *pagenumber* have the same meanings as for the `\l@sectionname` command.

The style files also define the actual `\tableofcontents` command, which typesets the contents title, marks the page headers and then calls the internal command `\@starttoc` command which performs the processing of the `.toc` file.

12.5.9   Index

The `theindex` environment sets up two column formatting and·typesets the index title. It also defines some useful skips and spaces. At the end of the environment single column typesetting is restored and the page is cleared.

12.5.10   Floats

The float section of `article` begins by specifying values for the float parameters described in the last chapter. Within a float environment the `\caption` command is defined which keeps the figure and table numbers up to date. It calls the internal command `\@makecaption{floatnumber}{captiontext}` which must be defined in the style file to actually typeset the caption. In `article` `\@makecaption` is defined using the `\long\def` command because its definition expands to more than one paragraph.

The float mechanism in LaTeX is quite general and other kinds of floats can be defined in addition to the usual `table` and `figure`. As part of the set-up, some useful internal commands are defined:

`\fps@floatname`
> the default float placement parameter, set to `tbp` in the standard styles.

`\fnum@floatname`
> which typesets the caption introducer. In `article`, `\fnum@float` is defined as `Figure \thefigure`

12.5.11   Title and abstract

The title and abstract definitions are straightforward. Footnotes are redefined to use the \fnsymbol printing sequence so that \thanks commands use the sequence listed in section 11.2.1 rather than numbers. The authors' names are set using a tabular environment. An interesting trick is the redefinition of \@topnum (the internal version of the \topnumber parameter) to zero to make sure that any floats on the title page do not end up at the top, above the title.

12.5.12   Page styles

A page style is used to define the contents of the page header and footer. When LaTeX encounters a \pagestyle{style} command in your document it attempts to execute a command \ps@style which must be defined in the style file. (In fact the command \ps@empty and \ps@plain for the {empty} and {plain} page styles are predefined in latex.tex, so do not need to be defined in the style.) The standard styles define two further styles: {headings} which puts the pagenumber and the section titles into the heading using uppercase italic letters, and {myheadings} which has the same initial effect but whose headers can be reprogrammed with the \markright and \markboth commands (see section 3.4.4).

The \ps@style command must define the following four commands: \@oddfoot, \@evenfoot, \@oddhead and \@evenhead. These commands are called by the page builder to actually typeset the head and foot of odd (right hand) and even (left hand) pages. In the standard styles, the footers are empty and the headers are constructed using the \rightmark and \leftmark commands that are defined by the LaTeX \markboth and \markright commands.

The sectioning commands call \@startsection as described above. One of the housekeeping functions performed by \@startsection is to call a command called \namemark where name is the name of the section (chapter, section, subsection and so on). If the command does not exist, LaTeX continues but you can define a command such as \sectionmark to get the section name and number into a running header.

12.5.13   Initialisation

The final part of article.sty sets up defaults for some LaTeX parameters. Arabic page numbering, a plain page style with no page headers and single column printing are specified. Usually \raggedbottom typesetting is used unless twosided printing as been selected in which case \flushbottom printing is necessary so that the both sides of a sheet will line up.

12.6   The report and book styles

The report and book styles are very similar to article, differing mainly in their handling of title pages and abstract, and in their default initialisations. book handles the declarations for the part section rather differently. Almost all of the above discussion applies equally well to these other two styles.

12.7   The `letter` style

The `letter` style is significantly different to the others, and is interesting in that it shows how little needs to be defined to make a working style file. The first thing to note is that there are no separate subsidiary style files to handle the different font commands. Instead, the font changing options are all handled directly within `letter.sty` using the usual `\ds@`*`option`* mechanism. The reason that the other styles split these commands off is the very limited amount of memory LaTeX has available for macro definitions. Having to hold a full set of definitions for all three sizes in the `article` style would strain TeX's capacity, so `article` only reads in the ones that it needs, but the letter style is much smaller so there is sufficient space for all the definitions. In addition, letter writers rarely define large sets of private commands, which again reduces the demands on macro memory.

Floats are not supported in letters, but LaTeX will complain if the float parameters are not defined in the style, so an arbitrary set of parameters must appear.

The letter commands are defined after the float parameters. The `letter.doc` file supplies instructions for customising these commands to local requirements. If you have a typeset heading for your letters that replaces the company notepaper, call it up as part of the definition of `\opening`.

`letter` defines a special page style called `{firstpage}` that is automatically set for the first page of a letter. This is usually used to insert telephone and fax numbers in the footer for page 1. Subsequent pages use `{plain}`, which is defined to put a page number in the bottom of the footer. An unusual skip of `0pt plus 0.00006fil` is defined for the top of the first page, which moves a short letter towards the center of the page. Some people dislike this visual effect when headed A4 notepaper is in use because it leaves a large blank space under the header.

The rest of `letter` is fairly conventional and the discussion of `article` above applies.

12.8   A few special effects

The problem with the standard styles is that they are rather, well, *standard*. Many books and papers have been typeset with them, and you might wish to make your documents look a little different. However, before wading in and changing everything look carefully at real typeset books and always try to follow, or even copy, the styles used there. The availability of cheap word processing and desktop publishing systems has resulted in a mass of cheap and nasty books and documents. If you are reading a book like this, it is likely that you have technical expertise with computers, but remember that technical knowledge does not necessarily assist the task of artistic design.

There are many useful style files available for free that implement new commands and commonly requested visual formatting tricks. You will find details on how to obtain these files in the next chapter. The following sections illustrate a few simple effects that I use in the style files for this and other books.

12.8.1   Globally disabling hyphenation

When typesetting posters that use very large type, or narrow column text with less than 30 characters on a line TEX's usually excellent hyphenation can become intrusive. The command \hyphenpenalty is used to insert a penalty at every hyphenation point on a line, and hyphenation may be switched off by setting it to infinity (10000) with the command \hyphenpenalty=10000.

12.8.2   Turning off leaders

The dotted lines used across a contents page are considered to be a little old fashioned by some publishers. One way to disable them is to rewrite all of the \l@*sectionname* commands that are used to typeset the contents entry, but a useful trick is to increase the internal parameter \@dotsep which defines the dot separation to \textwidth. This ensures that no dots ever appear, because the first dot is guaranteed to be outside of the text body.

12.8.3   Defining chapter-like units

The preface and forward of a book are typeset as individual mini-chapters. These commands define a \preface command will produce a chapter headed **Preface** and make an entry in the table of contents file:

```
\def\preface{\chapter*{\huge\sfb Preface}
\@mkboth{}{}
\addcontentsline{toc}{chapter}{Preface}}
```

12.8.4   Changing float captions

The standard float caption comprises the float name and number followed by a colon and the *text* parameter from the \caption command. These commands make captions like those in this book: the float name and number in bold sans-serif with no trailing colon. They are simple modifications of the commands copied from the standard styles.

```
%
% take the colon out of the captions
%
\long\def\@makecaption#1#2{
 \vskip 10pt
 \setbox\@tempboxa\hbox{{\bf #1} #2}
 \ifdim \wd\@tempboxa >\hsize \unhbox\@tempboxa\par \else \hbox
to\hsize{\hfil\box\@tempboxa\hfil}
 \fi}
%
% Make caption introducers bold sans-serif
%
\def\fnum@figure{\sfb Figure \thefigure}
```

```
\def\fnum@table{\sfb Table \thetable}
```

12.8.5 Changing contents entries

In the contents pages for this book chapter headings are typeset in bold sans-serif. This is done by copying the standard style's `\l@chapter` command which is used to typeset the entry and adding a font changing command:

```
%
% Make contents entries for \chapter bold sand serif
%
\def\l@chapter#1#2{\addpenalty{-\@highpenalty}%
   \vskip 1.0em plus\p@
   \@tempdima 1.5em
   \begingroup
     \parindent \z@ \rightskip \@pnumwidth
     \parfillskip -\@pnumwidth
     \sfb                               % change font
     \leavevmode
      \advance\leftskip\@tempdima
      \hskip -\leftskip
     #1\nobreak\hfil \nobreak\hbox to\@pnumwidth{\hss #2}\par
     \penalty\@highpenalty
   \endgroup}
```

12.8.6 How to make section headings hang back

Many modern books use wide pages with section headings that hang back into the left hand margin. You can get this effect by manipulating TeX's primitive `\leftskip` and `\rightskip` lengths within the section command. The standard styles define sectioning commands as

```
\def\section{\@startsection {section}{1}{\z@}%
             {-3.5ex plus-1ex minus -.2ex}%
             {2.3ex plus.2ex}{\reset@font\Large\bf}}
```

The final parameter to the `\@startsection` command is a set of declarations that are executed immediately before the section title is typeset, as described in section 12.5.7. Now the `\leftskip` and `\rightskip` registers are skip values that are automatically inserted at the start and end of every line, so if the commands

```
\leftskip=-2cm
\rightskip=0pt plus 1fil
```

are added immediately before the `\reset@font` command then the section title will outdent 2cm, and a spring will be placed on the right.

13

LaTeX past, present and future

This chapter is about the LaTeX add-ons and variants that have been developed and placed in the public domain by various public spirited individuals. It is in the nature of the subject that this information will go out of date rather quickly, so it would be unwise to treat this material as authoritative.

The generosity shown by computer people in making so much of their work freely available is a remarkable phenomenon, probably unmatched in any other sphere of professional activity. Armed with the information in the last chapter, you may write your own style files that would be useful to the wider community and this presents a marvellous opportunity to give back, and even gain a little fame. In section 13.2 there is some advice on how to obtain those style files which are not part of the standard distribution. If you get files from a network archive, you can also upload your own contributions which will then become available for all to share.

13.1 TeX and LaTeX history

The TeX project began in 1977 when Knuth received proofs for the second edition of his *Art of Computer Programming* [Knu69]. The new edition had been phototypeset using computers rather than hand set, and the mathematics spacing in particular was very poor. Knuth resolved to produce a typesetting system that would produce documents to the finest standards. The new system was also designed to be machine independent, both in terms of the host computer and the target phototypesetting machine. An early version (TeX78) was replaced by the present TeX system in about 1982, and the definitive description of the system, Knuth's TeXbook [Knu86a] was first published in 1984.

A freely available typesetting system needs freely available fonts to go with it, and Knuth also created the METAFONT system for designing characters. METAFONT is a programming language that can be used to describe the free-flowing curves from which typefaces may be constructed. Nearly all of the characters in this book are from the Computer Modern (CM) fonts designed by Knuth and drawn using METAFONT.

The TeX and METAFONT programs are written in a style Knuth calls 'literate programming'. The idea is to intermingle a typeset description of the program with the actual computer programming language code into a single document that is both the program and the description of the program. This new programming style is called WEB and has been applied to most of the main computer programming languages. A WEB file may be processed by TEX to produce a beautiful document, or it may be processed to produce just the computer language source code which can then be compiled in the normal way.

Knuth published a series of five volumes which comprise the user manuals for TEX using the plain format [Knu86a], METAFONT[Knu86c], the WEB source code for the two programs [Knu86b, Knu86d] and a description of the design and METAFONT source code for the CM fonts [Knu86e]. TEX and its relations are fascinating tools because they attempt to embody the *art* of good aesthetic design as well as the technical details. It turns out to be straightforward to design a new font in METAFONT, but extremely difficult to design an attractive and readable one. The more one uses TEX the more respect one gains for the generations of typographers who have evolved our present fonts and book styles.

TEX was quickly taken up by academics and others in the USA. In particular, the American Mathematical Society (AMS) was closely involved in the development of TEX and continues to support its development. A macro package called AMS-TEX was developed by Michael Spivak [Spi86] and is widely used by mathematicians. AMS-TEX provides new fonts and many new commands in the plain TEX style. Section 13.5 describes a fusion of AMS-TEX and LATEX which you can obtain for free.

Leslie Lamport's LATEX system [Lam86] was generally available by the mid-1980's. Many versions of latex.tex have been released, so you should check the date at the top of your latex.tex file. The version described in this book is Version 2.09, dated 18 March 1992. Versions with numbers prior to 2.09 are now completely obsolete, and versions of 2.09 dated before 1991 may not work with all of the extensions described in this chapter.

LATEX seems to be more dominant in Europe, probably because it became available just as TEX was becoming popular in Europe, whereas American users who had been using plain for some years tended to stick with it.

13.1.1 TEX version 3

The growing international use of TEX led to a small upgrade which allows fonts from other systems, to be used more easily. The original version of TEX made certain assumptions about which character number in a font corresponded to which symbol. For the standard alphabetic characters this is not a real restriction, but there is no universal standard for the numbering of mathematical symbols, and every font supplier has their own ordering. Knuth introduced the idea of a *virtual font* that maps a foreign font into TEX's scheme. At the same time, support for some foreign language features was improved and the hyphenation algorithm given a little more flexibility. Most users will not notice any difference between the old and new versions of TEX, except that a version 3 TEX format *must* set some new parameters, or the hyphenation will become over enthusiastic. If you find that your documents is clearly over hyphenated then you have a version mismatch. The most common symptom is that plural words are hyphenated at the end. If your version of LATEX does this then you should complain bitterly to your supplier or system manager. At the time of writing, TEX 3.0 has been around long enough to have supplanted most earlier versions, so you are unlikely to see this problem. Versions of LaTeX dated after the beginning of 1992 will work correctly with TeX 3.0 and the files described in this chapter.

13.2   How to get add-ons

Nearly all TeX systems include a copy of the standard LaTeX system as described in this book, but the extensions and style files described in the rest of this chapter have to be acquired from other sources. If you work in a University or for a large company, you may have access to computers connected to the world-wide Internet, and by far the easiest way of getting additional materials is through the network. Ideally, you need access to email, file transfers through ftp and the Internet news system.

If you cannot access the Internet, then try contacting your TeX supplier or join one of the User groups listed in section 13.11, who should be able to supply the necessary files. The rest of this section is for people that do have Internet access.

Many people find the Internet rather overwhelming at a first acquaintance. I strongly recommend that you get a copy of the document *Zen and the Art of the Internet: A Beginner's guide to the Internet* by Brendan P. Kehoe [Keh92], which is full of useful advice and information about Internet services. Copies of the booklet may be found in most large Internet archives, and since the booklet is written using TeX you should be able to format it and print it out. Of course, if you need this booklet you will need the help of a more experienced net user to retrieve it from the network...

The best way to navigate the Internet is to learn how to use the Archie network database system. Archie is a collection of computers spread around the world that know of about 1000 anonymous ftp archives. Every night Archie asks some of the archive sites about any new files they have acquired, and over the course of a week or two the entire database is updated in a rolling program. You can ask Archie to tell you where particular files are held, and you will quickly find the nearest archive site to you. You access Archie by `telnet`ing to an Archie site and logging in as `archie`.

If you do have access to the Internet News service, then you should subscribe to the conference `comp.text.tex` which carries a high volume of traffic on TeX matters. Around 30% of the messages concern LaTeX. There are several large repositories of TeX material on the Internet, and most of them allow access *via* mail servers and FTP. In the United Kingdom the major site is `tex.ac.uk` (`134.151.40.18`) which allows anonymous ftp and has a mail server address `texserver@tex.ac.uk`. In the USA, `ymir.claremont.edu` (`134.173.4.23`) allows anonymous ftp and mail service through `MAILSERV@ymir.claremont.edu`. In Germany, the machine `rusinfo.rus.uni-stuttgart.de` (`129.69.1.12`) allows anonymous ftp. This machine will have the latest versions of the Mainz extensions described in section 13.7, as well as the latest versions of emTeX, which is widely considered to be the best TeX implementation for the IBM-PC. This machine also holds hyphenation patterns for European languages.

13.3   Useful extensions and auxiliary programs

The sections that follow describe two variants of LaTeX — International LaTeX and
$\mathcal{AMS}$-LaTeX — as well as style files and programs that I have found useful. This
is not a complete guide. There are over 350 style files in the Internet TeX archive
and space does not allow more than a small sample to be described. However, the
Mainz extensions subsume many of the earlier style files, so you should concentrate
on getting these items first.

13.4   International LaTeX

The LaTeX style files are written for American English users. Words like `Chapter`
and `Appendix` are written into the definitions of the sectioning commands, and the
`\today` macro uses an American format date. International LaTeX (ILaTeX), written
by Joachim Schrod, defines a series of macros like `\chaptername` and `\appedixname`
whose default values correspond to the standard English names used in this book,
but which can be redefined in a document to convert it to say, French or German,
without rewriting the original style file. Previously a plethora of individual styles
have been written to support European language variants of the standard styles.
The ideas in ILaTeX have been incorporated into the latest versions of LaTeX 2.09,
so you may already have the necessary files. Check your `article.doc` file for
internationalisation comments to find out.

13.5 $\mathcal{AMS}$-LaTeX

$\mathcal{AMS}$-LaTeX version 1.1 was released in August 1991 and represents an ambitious
attempt to combine the extra mathematical typesetting capabilities of $\mathcal{AMS}$-TeX
with LaTeX. It uses the new font selection scheme discussed below and provides
an `[amstex]` document style option that defines a host of new commands which
amongst other things improves the spacing of LaTeX's maths accents, multiple integral signs, roots and continued fractions, allows multi-line subscripts and superscripts and provides extremely flexible equation numbering and alignment. $\mathcal{AMS}$-
LaTeX fixes many of the criticisms of LaTeX maths display handling, especially the
rather restricted equation labelling facilities. The bad news is that $\mathcal{AMS}$-LaTeX
is very large, and will almost certainly require a big TeX implementation to run
satisfactorily. $\mathcal{AMS}$-LaTeX comes with a manual that describes the new commands.

13.6   Beyond LaTeX 2.09

LaTeX has continued to evolve throughout the 1980's and recently Lamport has
agreed that an upgraded version will be produced by a team which he will chair,
but led by Frank Mittelbach and Rainer Schöpf of Mainz University in Germany.
Mittelbach and Schöpf have originated a powerful set of extensions to LaTeX 2.09,
most notably the new font selection scheme used in $\mathcal{AMS}$-LaTeX, and are thus well
qualified to take over the maintenance of LaTeX. This work has now evolved into

the LATEX 3.0 project which hopes to add functionality to LATEX but perhaps more importantly systematise and document the internal structure and provide a new interface for style file writers. At the time of writing, test versions of key parts of LATEX 3.0 have been demonstrated, but a general release is not expected for at least two years. It will take time for the new system, which will differ in many small respects from the existing LATEX to spread, so LATEX 2.09 is likely to be in widespread use until at least the mid-1990's.

13.7   The Mainz extensions to LATEX 2.09

The good news is that the main new functions (as opposed to the new style file interface) of LATEX 3.0 are available now and can be used with LATEX 2.09. There are six extension packages:

New font selection scheme

this extends LATEX's font selection mechanism to support any available font equally, and makes font family, size and style commands independent of each other, so that for instance font size can be changed without automatically resetting to \rm.

Enhanced tabular and array environment

extra column formatting commands are added to allow font changing declarations to be automatically inserted and more flexible \parbox formatting

Enhanced multicolumn output

allows three or more column typesetting with automatic balancing of the heights of the columns, and changes in column layout for a single page

Multicolumn footnotes on the right

gathers together footnotes in a multicolumn environment and places them under the rightmost column

Theorem styles

Enhances theorem environments to use a *theorem style* which by analogy with the LATEX page style programs the layout of a theorem.

New verbatim implementation

The LATEX theorem environment has a finite capacity (of about five pages in the standard sized TEX). This new implementation can cope with arbitrarily long verbatim sections, and adds a command to read in a file in verbatim mode.

A feature of these extensions is that they have been written in a way that gives the user *hooks* into the internal structure. For instance the new verbatim style calls a command at the beginning of each line, and by redefining this command the user can achieve special effects, such as adding a line number to each line of an included file. LATEX itself has many such hooks, but they are undocumented and unstructured, so it is very difficult to use them. A major goal of LATEX 3.0 is to provide hooks like this in a consistent fashion.

13.8   Other useful style files

Apart from the Mainz files, I find these styles to be indispensible:

`ukdate.sty` redefines the `\today` command to print dates in the form

> Tuesday 7th July 1992.
>
> Also defines commands `\st`, `\nd`, `\rd` and `\th` to typeset the suffices, and `\dayofweek`.

`A4.sty` resets the page size to A4 using margins that keep the text legible by restricting the number of characters on a line to about 70. A `\Widemargins` command opens up the margins even more to allow reasonable size marginal notes.

`EPIC` enhances the LATEX picture environment with many new commands including `\dottedline`, `\dashline` and `\drawline` which draws lines between a sequence of coordinate pairs without needing explicit slope calculations.

`fancyheadings.sty` adds commands for headings with a left, centre and right part which may be underlined, and may extend over the margins. Allows you to have different headings on chapter pages.

`boxedminipage.sty` adds the `boxedminipage` environment which is identical to `minipage` except that a box is drawn around the outside. Many of the figures in this book use `boxedminipage` to highlight the source code.

`breakcit.sty` The standard `\cite` command produces a typeset citation that can not be broken across lines. This can be a real problem if you make use of citation commands that include multiple references. `breakcite` redefines `\cite` so that line breaking is allowed.

13.9   Useful auxiliary programs

`delatex` If you pass a LATEX document through a spelling checker it will throw up many 'unknown' words which are in fact LATEX commands. `delatex` goes through your file and removes all of the LATEX commands so that you should be left with just your text which can then be safely spell checked. `delatex` is also useful for producing versions of your file for text-only environments such as computer bulletin boards.

`makeindex` LATEX has only rather rudimentary facilities for typesetting indices. The `makeindex` (or `makeindx` on MS-DOS systems) comprises a style file that defines index making commands, and a program that takes the output of the LATEX `\index` commands and sorts it and formats it ready for inclusion during the next run, performing the same kind of functions for indexing as BIBTEX does for citation. `makeindx` has its own syntax which may be used in the `\index` command parameter: A ! character is used to mark a sub-entry and an @ character may be used to separate the sort key and the actual text of the index entry.

tgrind is a TeX version of the `vgrind` pretty printer program found on many Unix system. It understands C, Pascal, FORTRAN and many other languages, and will typeset keywords in bold, comments in italics, strings in teletype and so on. It is quite easy to extend `tgrind` to cope with new languages. The original release of `tgrind` was for plain TeX only: as well as the main `tgrind` package you will need a copy of `tgrind.sty` which is a LaTeX version of the formatting macros.

TeXcad and `xfig` The picture environment is very tiresome to use if the position of every object must be calculated and typed in. TeXcad is a mouse or keyboard driven program for IBM-PC compatibles that allows you to draw a picture on the screen and then save it as a complete LaTeX picture environment, ready for inclusion in your file. TeXcad can also read most pictures in, which means you can use a text editor to modify a picture and then make some more visual changes with the mouse. A recent version of the program supports the `\bezier` command and a new version for X-windows is in development. Most of the figures in this book were drawn with TeXcad.

`xfig` is a well known drawing program for computers running the X-windows system. A converter program `transfig` can translate from `xfig`'s native data format to LaTeX picture mode, but not the other way.

Converters from word processors to LaTeX Converting from an existing word processor format to LaTeX is unlikely to ever be automatic, so you should treat these programs as tools to perform most of the housekeeping, not the last word in conversion.

program	source format
wp2latex	Word perfect
wd2latex	MS-Word
pcwtex	PC-Write
RUNOFF-to-TeX	Runoff
tr2latex	troff

13.10   Using other fonts

There is no reason why TeX should be limited to the `cmr` series fonts. Essentially, TeX can use any fonts for which `.tfm` files are available. This includes Postscript fonts and native fonts for some laser printers, as well as any font which has been produced with METAFONT. Making use of such fonts within LaTeX requires more work. The NFSS font scheme makes it straightforward to access these alien fonts from with LaTeX, but it turns out that ligatures and maths characters have different `\symbol` codes in the postscript world from the `cmr` fonts. The extensions in TeX 3.0 offer a mechanism for harmonising these font families, but at the time of writing the necessary changes to LᴬTEX have not been made. Many people prefer the Postscript fonts to the Computer Modern family, so this situation may well be remedied soon.

13.11   User groups

The best way to get the most out of a complex system like TEX is to join a user group and benefit from the expertise of others, as well as keeping up to date with developments in the TEX world. The TEX Users Group (TUG) is the main international group. They publish a journal called TUGBOAT and market various TEX related packages and services. They may be contacted at

> TEX Users Group
> P.O. Box 9506
> Providence, RI 02940
> USA

Electronic mail for TUG may be sent to `TUG@Math.AMS.com`

There are many thriving national groups. In the United Kingdom, *ukTEXug* meets every few months and produces a newsletter called Baskerville. They may be contacted through

> Geeti Granger
> Text Processing Department
> John Wiley and Sons Ltd.
> Baffins Lane
> Chichester
> West Sussex
> PO19 1UD

Electronic mail enquiries may be addressed to `uktug-enquiries@tex.ac.uk`: please remember to include your postal address if you want membership details.

Other national groups include DANTE in Germany, GUTenberg in France and the NTG for Dutch speaking users. There are also groups in Japan, Scandinavia, Mexico and Eastern Europe. TUG should be able to tell you about user group activity in your area.

A

Hints on running LaTeX

A.1 Getting LaTeX

Although LaTeX and TeX are in the public domain, individual implementations
may not be. Commercial versions of the system are available from several vendors:
contact TUG at the address given at the end of the last chapter for details.

Public domain versions are available for Unix, VMS, MS-DOS, TOPS-20, Macintosh, the Atari and the Amiga. The servers listed in the last chapter are a good
place to start looking, but please remember that TeX is a very large system and
observe good network etiquette when downloading.

A.2 How to run LaTeX

Every LaTeX system should include a copy of the *Local Guide* that has instructions
for your particular implementation. This file is called `local.tex` and will be found
in your inputs directory. Unfortunately, in the vast majority of installations this
document is not updated from Lamport's original text, which is specific to the
Ultrix (DEC Unix) implementation at SRI. There is a surprising amount of variation
between different implementations, so I can only offer some hints that might apply
to you. The best thing is to get hold of the manuals for your system, or ask someone
else who knows how to drive it.

On most systems LaTeX is run by issuing the command `latex` *filename* to the
operating system. Failing that, try `tex &lplain` *filename* which starts raw TeX
with the `lplain` format.

There is a special version of TeX called INITeX that is used for building new
format files. Instructions for building a new LaTeX format may be found on page 123.
The command to start INITeX is usually just `initex`, but on the emTeX IBM PC
implementation it is called by typing `tex -i`.

There is wide variation in the design and naming of DVI drivers, and you should
consult the documentation or another user. Assuming that you are trying to produce output for a Postscript printer, try `dvi` *filename* first, failing that try `dvi2ps`
filename. On some Unix systems the command `lpr -d` *filename* will directly
print a `.dvi` file without any need to explicitly run the DVI driver.

Even when you have worked out how to start the DVI driver you should still ask
to see the manual as many DVI drivers can do useful things like including graphics,
printing two pages side by side and so on.

There is similar wide variation in DVI previewers. If you have a workstation
running the X-windows system try `xdvi` *filename*. If you have a VMS workstation
running the VWS windowing system try `dvidis` *filename*. On MS-DOS, `dviscr`
filename might help.

Printing commands are so varied that it is unlikely that your particular command
corresponds to any of these, but on Unix try `lpr -d` *filename*`.dvi` or `lpr -l`
filename`.ps` if you have a postscript file produced by a DVI driver. On VMS try
`lprint` *filename*`.ps` or `print/form=tex` *filename*`.ps`. On some MS-DOS systems
`spr` *filename*`.ps` works, and on others you should simply copy the contents of the
print file directly to the printer with `copy` *printfile* `prn`. You should use copy
rather than the regular `print` command because graphics files may contain binary
information that will be truncated by `print`.

B

Error messages

Simple errors can cause TeX to generate intimidating error messages. In point of fact, if you get an error message from TeX that you fully understand you should count yourself lucky. However you do always get at least a message and the line number at which TeX ran into trouble, and this is usually close to the cause of the problem. However, TeX also regurgitates the definition of the macro that is currently being processed. If you wrote the macro yourself then it might be useful to be given all this, but LaTeX macros are often very complex, and you may well be presented with several lines of complete gobledegook. In general it best to ignore nearly all of this.

Most errors arise from simple spelling mistakes. For instance, if you incorrectly capitalise \LaTeX you will get an error message similar to

```
! Undefined control sequence
1.12 \Latex
?
```

This tells you that TeX encountered a control word not in its symbol table at line 12 of the outermost file being processed.

Probably the next most common error is to use a maths mode command in text mode. In this case TeX inserts an extra $ before the command in question. Of course this may not be very helpful. TeX also stops and tells you what it's done

```
! Missing $ inserted
1.14 ... $
          \alpha
?
```

B.1   Responding to errors

Normally when TeX detects an error it will stop after issuing the error message and prompt with a ? If you type a carriage return TeX will then continue until it finds another error. Sometimes TeX will get stuck on a single error, and then you should type an X which forces TeX to exit.

If you type H then TeX will try to help you with a longer error message.

If you type R at the prompt then TeX enters *batchmode* when it will run non-stop even if it finds errors. You can get the same effect by inserting a \batchmode command in your file. Remember that the screen output is always copied to the

.log file, so you can peruse the errors afterwards. If you type Q (for quiet) then TeX enters batchmode but only sends further messages to the log file

Some implementations of TeX allow you to type an E which will then start up a text editor with the cursor at the point of the error. You can then make corrections and exit the error after which TeX will continue processing.

B.2   Warnings

Some LaTeX messages are warnings, and do not cause TeX to halt and prompt for instructions. The most common ones are the Overfull \hbox type messages that every TeX user quickly becomes familiar with. You will also be warned if you reference an undefined label or citation, multiply define a label, try to plot an oval that is too small, or if a marginal note has to be shifted so as to avoid overlapping another note.

B.3   Error messages

This section gives a complete list of the errors reported by LaTeX version 2.09, with advice on how to correct them. Also listed here are some of TeX's more common error messages that you may occasionally see. There are some messages that are not in this list, but they will arise from some catastrophe so deep inside LaTeX that an explanation of the message's meaning is unlikely to help you.

In such circumstances, first fix any preceding errors (because knock-on errors are common) and then if it still doesn't go away look carefully at your file in the vicinity of the message line number. You may wish to take a copy of the offending document file and remove parts of it until the error disappears, which will give you some idea of what is causing it. Almost certainly a little thought will reveal the error to be a simple typing mistake, and looking at the file for a few minutes can be quicker than slicing it up methodically chasing bugs. Remember the old joke about the engineer who had a flat tyre, and swapped all the wheels round to make sure it wasn't a bug in the suspension...

Bad \line or \vector argument
:   You have asked for a slope which is not available on the LaTeX line drawing font.

Bad math environment delimiter
:   You have unbalanced braces or maths mode delimiters.

Bad use of \\
:   You have tried to end a line when TeX is in vertical mode within a center, flushleft or flushright environment.

\begin{*environment1*} ended by \end{*environment2*}
:   You have unbalanced environment delimiters, or a misspelt environment name.

Can be used only in preamble
:   The highlighted command must appear before the \begin{document}

Command name '\name' already used
> You have used a \new... command to define a name that already exists. Use \renew... instead, or choose another name. Note that defining an environment *environmentname* creates internal commands called *environmentname* and \end*environmentname*.

Counter too large
> One of the \alph, \Alph or \fnsymbol counter printing commands have been passed a counter with too large a number. Could be triggered by a large number of \thanks commands or a very long enumerate list.

Double subscript
> subscripts must be nested: use x_{y_z} not x_y_z

Double superscript
> superscripts must be nested: use x^{y^z} not x^y^z

Environment *environmentname* undefined
> Perhaps you can't spell the environment name.

Extra alignment tab has been changed to \cr
> There are more & separated fields in a row of an array or tabular environment than you declared in the column formatting parameter.

Extra }, or forgotten $
> You have badly nested braces or maths mode characters.

Float(s) lost
> The output routine has detected that you requested a float from inside a parbox or minipage environment. Since the error is only detected when floats are output, no useful indication can be given of where the error occurred and you will have to scan your file to find the offending table environment, figure environment or \marginpar command.

Font *name* not loaded: Not enough room left
> You have asked for more fonts than TeX can cope with. Process the document in separate parts using \includeonly or reduce the number of fonts.

I can't find file *name*. Please type another input file name
> TeX cannot find your main file, a style file or a file that you have \input or \included. You can type in a new file name, or on some operating systems you can type cntrl-C to stop TeX. There are systems (MS-DOS amongst them) that will keep asking you this question until you give it the name of a real file. If you respond null, press return and then type a cntrl-C you will usually get to TeX's interactive prompt from which you can type X to stop TeX.

Illegal character in array arg
> Check the column formatting parameters listed in section 7.2.2.

Illegal parameter number in definition of *newcommand*

You have used a # sign inside the definition of a command incorrectly, or attempted to nest command definitions.

Misplaced alignment tab character &

An ampersand & has appeared outside of an **array** or **tabular** environment.

Missing \begin{document}

Printing commands were found before the **begin{document}**. Only declarations and spaces are allowed in the preamble.

Missing @-exp in array arg

You have an @ column formatting parameter with no following expression in braces.

Missing p-arg in array arg

You have an p column formatting parameter with no following expression in braces.

Missing $ inserted

You used a maths mode command without entering maths mode first. Remember that most of the non-alphanumeric symbols in Chapter 5 are maths mode commands.

No such counter

Perhaps you can't spell the counter name, or perhaps you have defined the counter in an \included file.

Not in outer par mode

You have a float defining command in maths mode, or in a parbox or **minipage** environment.

Paragraph ended before *object* **was complete**

You have tried to pass more than one paragraph to a parameter of a normal (not \long) definition.

\pushtabs and \poptabs don't match

You have unbalanced commands within a single **tabbing** environment. You cannot save tab setting across **tabbing** environments — every \pushtabs must have a matching \poptabs before the \end{tabbing} command.

\scriptfont *font-name* **is undefined**

You have tried to use an unusual font in maths mode with issuing a \load command first. See page 87.

\scriptscriptfont *font-name* **is undefined**

You have tried to use an unusual font in maths mode with issuing a \load command first. See page 87.

Something's wrong--perhaps a missing \item

You have misused a `list` environment or one of the many environments defined in terms of it. A completely empty `quote` environment will trigger this error.

\textfont *font-name* is undefined

You have tried to use an unusual font in maths mode with issuing a `\load` command first. See page 87.

Tab overflow

You have tried to set more than about 12 tab stops.

TeX capacity exceeded, sorry

Probably there is a simple error in your file that caused TeX to run out of room, such as defining a recursive command. You might really have run out of room if you have a large picture environment (the sequence of pictures in Chapter 11 is enough to break a normal sized TeX), or if you have a very long `verbatim` environment. If you really need more space, ask if there is a big TeX implementation available and try that instead. If the problem does not go away, you probably have a typing error, and you may have trouble finding it (sorry).

There's no line here to end

You have tried to end a line when TeX is in vertical mode. If you need to force a line end, say after an optional argument to an `\item` command try using `~\\` which adds one line comprising an invisible space. If you just want some more space, use a `\vspace` command instead.

This may be a LaTeX bug

Probably LaTeX has become disoriented after being asked to continue from another error. If this is the *first* error message to appear, then congratulations, your name may eventually appear in `latex.bug`.

Too deeply nested

You have more than four nested lists (in the standard styles). Some styles may allow more.

Too many unprocessed floats

LaTeX has been probably been inhibited from outputting floats because the combination of float parameters (section 11.11) and float placement commands have conspired together. This error may also occur if you have more than about 18 `\marginpar` commands on a page.

Undefined control sequence

perhaps you can't spell the name of a command, or you have tried to use an `\item` or `\caption` command outside of the a `figure` or `table` environment.

Undefined tab position

You need to define some more tabs positions, or modify your tabbing commands.

You can't use 'macro parameter character #' in *name* mode
> A # character appeared in normal text. Use \# instead.

`\< in mid line`
> `\<` may only appear at the beginning of a line.

B.4   Warning messages

Warning messages do not cause TEX to stop, and in some cases you will be happy to ignore them. However, it is a good idea to check the log file *before* you send your paper off to the editor because an embarrassing warning about a non-existent citation may have scrolled past whilst you were not concentrating.

The majority of warning messages you see will be `Overfull \hbox ...` messages that can be tiresome to clear up because an overrun of a few points can sometimes be difficult to see on a printed proof. Try using the [draft] document style option to place a large bar next to the offending lines. Please don't get into the habit of ignoring overfull box messages. A wobbly right margin is a sure sign of a LATEX user who needs more pride in his work[1].

Citation *key* on page *pagenumber* undefined
> You need to run BIBTEX to get your references up to date

Float larger than \textheight
> You have an overlong `figure` or `table` environment.

Label *key* multiply defined
> You have used the same label more than once

Label(s) may have changed. Rerun to get cross-references right
> Since LATEX uses a two pass system to build references (see page 35) multiple runs may be needed before the labels settle down.

Marginpar on page *pagenumber* moved
> Two marginal notes would have overlapped but have been moved apart.

No *font* typeface in this size, using *newfont*
> Some fonts, such as \tt\tiny are not defined so another will be substituted.

Oval too small
> The oval specified has been drawn, but looks bad because the circular corners overlap.

Overfull \hbox ...
> TEX could not find a good linebreak, and has been forced to leave some text hanging out into the margin.

---

[1]As are right quotes appearing at the start of quotations (leave that double-quote key alone), italics running into neighbouring roman type (use an italic correction) and interword hyphens being used for punctuation.

`Overfull \vbox ...`

TEX could not find a good pagebreak, and has been forced to leave some text running off the bottom of the page.

`Reference` *key* `on page` *pagenumber* `undefined`

You have `\ref` or `\pageref`ed a label that does not exist.

`Underfull \hbox ...`

By using consecutive `\\` commands or the `\linebreak` command you have persuaded TEX to typeset consecutive vertical spaces. If you need extra vertical space, use the optional argument to `\\` or a `\vspace` command.

`Underfull \vbox ...` TEX has made a page with large spaces between the paragraphs and section headings. Try rearranging your text, or give TEX some hints with a `\pagebreak` command.

command `in maths mode`

You have used an illegal maths mode command.

Bibliography

[Ame91]   American Mathematical Society. $\mathcal{AMS}$-LaTeX *Version 1.1 User's Guide*, August 1991.

[Doo]   Michael Doob. *A Gentle Introduction to TeX*. University of Manitoba, version 1.0.

[ISO80]   ISO. *Second DP 7185—Specification for the Computer Programming Language Pascal*. International Standards Organisation, 1980.

[Keh92]   Brendan P. Kehoe. *Zen and the Art of the Internet, A beginner's guide to the Internet*. Widener University, first edition, January 1992.

[Knu69]   Donald E. Knuth. *Seminumerical Algorithms*, volume 2 of *The Art of Computer Programming*. Addison Wesley, 1969.

[Knu86a] Donald E. Knuth. *The TeXbook*, volume A of *Computers and Typesetting*. Addison Wesley, 1986.

[Knu86b] Donald E. Knuth. *TeX: the program*, volume B of *Computers and Typesetting*. Addison Wesley, 1986.

[Knu86c] Donald E. Knuth. *The* METAFONT*book*, volume C of *Computers and Typesetting*. Addison Wesley, 1986.

[Knu86d] Donald E. Knuth. METAFONT*: the program*, volume D of *Computers and Typesetting*. Addison Wesley, 1986.

[Knu86e] Donald E. Knuth. *Computer Modern Typefaces*, volume E of *Computers and Typesetting*. Addison Wesley, 1986.

[Lam86]   L. Lamport. LaTeX *user's guide & reference manual*. Addison Wesley, 1986.

[SL91]   Raymond Seroul and Silvio Levy. *A Beginner's Book of TeX*. Springer-Verlag, 1991.

[Sno92]   Wynter Snow. *TeX for the Beginner*. Addison-Wesley, 1992.

[Spi86]   Michael D. Spivak. *The Joy of TeX*. The American Mathematical Society, 1986.

Index

ELLIS HORWOOD SERIES IN COMPUTERS AND THEIR APPLICATIONS
Series Editor: IAN CHIVERS, Senior Analyst, The Computer Centre, King's College, London, and formerly Senior Programmer and Analyst, Imperial College of Science and Technology, University of London

ELLIS HORWOOD SERIES IN COMPUTER COMMUNICATIONS AND NETWORKING
Series Editor: R.J. DEASINGTON, Principal Consultant, PA Consulting Group, Edinburgh, UK